Red **Line** 3

Das Trainingsbuch

von
Pauline Ashworth

Klett Lerntraining

Zu diesem Trainingsbuch gehört eine Audio-CD. Mit ihrer Hilfe lernst du, Englisch besser zu verstehen. Die Texte sind im Buch mit dem Symbol gekennzeichnet. Wenn du die Diktate und Lückendiktate schreibst, benutze die Pausentaste, um Zeit zum Schreiben zu haben. Viel Erfolg!

Sprecher: Breakspeare, Jane; Ellmann, Vanessa; Ellmann, Alison; Khalil, Louai; Martin, Benjamin; Turner, Adrian; Vollmer, Amelie; Vollmer, Dominik; Vollmer, Marie Louise; Walker, Amy; Walker, Zack
Produktion: Ton in Ton Medienhaus, Stuttgart

Bibliografische Information der Deutschen Nationalbibliothek
Die Deutsche Nationalbibliothek verzeichnet diese Publikation in der Deutschen Nationalbibliografie; detaillierte bibliografische Daten sind im Internet über http://dnb.dnb.de abrufbar.

Auflage 6 | 2015

Redaktion: form & inhalt verlagsservice Martin H. Bredol/Linda Strehl
Illustrationen: Lars Benecke, Hannover: S. 60; Susanne Bochem, Mainz: S. 60; Naomi Fearn, Berlin; Christian Hansen, Berlin: S. 60, 86, 111; Elsie Lennox, London: S. 73; David Norman, Meerbusch: S. 13, 41, 60, 86; Carolin Ina Schröter, Berlin: S. 86, 111; Birgit Tanck, Hamburg: S. 86; Katja Wesner; Fellbach: S. 33, 45, 48, 49, 60, 83, 86, 111, 113, 119; Steffen Wolff, Düsseldorf: S. 13; Dorothe Wolters, Köln: S. 88.
Umschlaggestaltung: Koma Amok, Stuttgart
Umschlagfotos: Corbis (Tim Pannel), Düsseldorf; Mauritius Images GmbH
Satz: klartext, Heidelberg
Reproduktion: Meyle + Müller GmbH + Co. KG, Pforzheim
Druck: Grafisches Centrum Cuno GmbH & Co. KG, Calbe (Saale)

Printed in Germany
ISBN 978-3-12-929977-7

Inhalt

Unit 3

Skills workshop 3

Test practice B

Unit 4

Skills workshop 4

Revision B

Unit 5

Skills workshop 5

Test practice C

Lösungen

Unit 1

Sportarten

1 Sieh dir die Bilder an und beschrifte sie. Welche Sportarten zeigen sie?

1. 

a) ____________________

b) ____________________

c) ____________________

→ f____________________

2. 

a) ____________________

b) ____________________

→ t____________________

3. 

a) ____________________

b) ____________________

→ s____________________

4. 

a) ____________________

→ r____________________

2 Löse die Worträtsel auf und ergänze das richtige Wort neben den Beschreibungen.

cocah **sloer** **freeeer** **rorcse** **tras** **fruser**

1. He can send players off the pitch. ________________
2. This person can stand up on a board on the water. ________________
3. This is a very good sportsperson. ________________
4. This person trains a team. ________________
5. This is the person who hasn't won. ________________
6. He or she gets the goals. ________________

3 Ein Fußballspiel. Lies den Text und setze die Verben an der passenden Stelle ein.

hit **kick** **play fairly** **score** **substitute** **tackle**

I'm City's best fan. I always go to the matches and get there early. Today we're playing Brighton but I don't like them. They always play hard and they never ________________. When they ________________, they always go for the knees and not for the ball. In fact I often think they ________________ our players more often than they get the ball. When the referee isn't looking, they often ________________ our best players, too, and then we need to ________________ them before they are tired. Our players are often too scared to ________________ a goal or even to go near the net – and that's just while they are warming up.

Synonyme

4 Verbinde diese Synonyme durch eine Linie miteinander.

spare	plan
chat	thing
article	zero
arrangement	extra
nil	talk

Tipp Je mehr englische Wörter du lernst, desto mehr mit ähnlicher oder gleicher Bedeutung kommen dazu. Manchmal hilft es, wenn du solche Wörter zusammen lernst!

Verben

5 Suche aus dem Buchstabengitter neun Verben heraus und ordne sie ihrer Übersetzung zu.

werden to ____________

verabreden ____________

klingen ____________

sich fühlen ____________

passen ____________

sich beschweren ____________

kaputtmachen ____________

c	o	m	p	l	a	i	n	e
s	r	e	p	o	r	t	t	h
f	n	h	d	g	r	a	u	q
q	d	m	v	m	a	t	c	h
o	v	s	o	u	n	d	h	b
b	f	a	i	m	g	n	y	r
b	e	c	o	m	e	u	w	e
l	e	r	k	z	z	k	p	a
c	l	x	j	t	h	a	n	k

sich bedanken ____________ berichten ____________

Die Bedeutung neuer Wörter erschließen

6 Übersetze zunächst die Wörter. Welche ähnlichen Wörter kennst Du? Vielleicht auch ein weiteres Wort aus dem Wortfeld oder ein ähnliches Wort im Französischen – oder handelt es sich um ein zusammengesetztes Wort?

feeling	Gefühl	to feel – fühlen
to agree	______	______
lonely	______	______
tradition	______	______
tiring	______	______
home-made	______	______
happily	______	______
hot chocolate	______	______
foggy	______	______

Ein Profil

7 Ergänze die rechts angegebenen Wörter am richtigen Platz.

______: 14
______: 5 feet 8 ______
______: 8 ______ 5 pounds
______: 7th July

Likes: swimming, ______

inches
stone
height
weight
rugby
birthday
age

Präpositionen mit Substantiven

8 Welche Präpositionen fehlen in den Sätzen? Trage sie ein.

What's the name _______ your favourite tennis player? Mine is Andy Murray. I've seen him play tennis _______ TV a few times and I even saw him _______ a shop ______ London once. But next week ______ Saturday I'm going to watch him play _______ Wimbledon. The game starts _______ 3 o'clock _______ the afternoon and I'm really looking forward to it. I'm going with a friend _______ my tennis club and I hope it doesn't rain. Not that it ever rains _______ London, of course!

Wichtige Wendungen

9 Bilde sechs verschiedene Sätze und ordne sie der richtigen Überschrift zu.

Sorry, I think	planned on Wednesday?
That's what	you're wrong.
Have you got anything	other plans.
I know what	you mean.
What are you	I think, too.
Sorry, I've got	doing at the weekend?

agreeing and disagreeing:

____

____

____

arranging to meet:

____

____

____

Wiederholung: die einfache Form der Gegenwart

Das ***simple present*** verwendest du,

– wenn etwas immer wieder passiert oder immer wahr ist:

I often **watch** football.
She doesn't **play** rugby.

– wenn du ein Geschehen wiedergibst:

They **get up** early and **go** skiing while the snow is good.

Signalwörter: always, usually, often, never, sometimes, every (day/month/year)

Aussage	Verneinung
I **love** swimming. She **likes** football.	I **don't like** football. He **doesn't like** rugby.
Fragen	**Kurzantwort**
Do you **train** often? **Does** he **help** you? What **do** you **like?**	Yes, I **do.** No, he **doesn't.**

To be und ***have got*** sind Hilfsverben und haben **kein *do*** oder ***does*** in der Frage oder Verneinung:

Are you hungry?
We haven't got a ball.

10 Verbinde die Fragen mit den passenden Antworten.

Which sport do you like best?	Yes, he does.
Are you good at table tennis?	No, I'm not.
Do you want to play now?	Table tennis.
Have you got a ball?	Yes, I do.
Does Jim have a ball?	No, I haven't.

11 Interview mit einem Tennisspieler. Bilde aus den angegebenen Wörtern vollständige Sätze.

how often – you – to train – ?

____

I – to train – three times a week

____

to be – your parents – good at sport – ?

____

yes *(short answer)* / my dad – to be – very good at tennis, too

____

your father – to help – you – ?

____

yes – he – often – to practise – with me

____

12 Gedanken eines Fussballspielers. Ergänze die richtige Formen der Verben.

I ______________ (like) Ann and I ______________ (love) football but I ______________ (not/have) time for both. So what can I do? ______________ (Ann/play) football? No, ______________ *(short answer)*, but she ______________ (play) hockey. I ______________ (not/play) hockey but I ______________ (have) an idea. Ann's friend, Sophie, ______________ (play) football. And ______________ (she/be) nice, too?

Yes, she is.

Wiederholung: die Verlaufsform der Gegenwart

Das ***present progressive*** verwendest du, um auszudrücken, dass etwas gerade passiert. Man bildet das *present progressive* mit einer Form von ***to be*** und der ***ing*-Form** des Verbs.

Signalwörter: Look! now, just, at the moment, today

Aussage	**Verneinung**
I'**m** just **doing** my homework. They **are eating** at the moment.	He **isn't watching** TV. We **aren't winning** now.
Fragen	**Kurzantwort**
Are you **sitting** on the bus? What **is** he **doing** now?	Yes, I **am.**/No, I'**m not.**

13 Schau dir die Bilder an und vervollständige die Lücken.

1. What ______________________ (do) now?

They ____________________________ (not/play tennis).

They ______________________.

2. What ______________________ (do) at the moment?

She ______________________________ (not/play rugby).

She ______________________________________.

3. ____________________________________ tennis?

____

____

4. ______________________________ (walk)?

____

____

Wiederholung: einfache Form der Gegenwart und Verlaufsform

Das ***simple present*** verwendest du, um auszudrücken,	Das ***present progressive*** verwendest du,
– dass etwas regelmäßig passiert oder nicht passiert: It often **rains** in England. – dass etwas eine Tatsache ist: I **like** football. I **don't understand.**	– wenn gerade etwas passiert: Look! We**'re winning** the match. What **are** you **doing** now? We **aren't meeting** today.
Signalwörter: always, often, never, sometimes, usually	Signalwörter: Look! now, at the moment, today

14 John ruft Gemma an, die gerade bei einem Kricketspiel zusieht. Ergänze die richtige Zeitform des Verbs.

John: Hi Gemma. How ________________ (it/go) now?

Gemma: Oh, fine. We ________________________ (just/have) a picnic.

John: No, I mean in the game. __________________ (they/play) well?

Gemma: Oh, the game! I don't know. I _______________________ (not/ understand) it at all. The man _____________ (hit) the ball and then sometimes he __________ (run) and scores but sometimes he _______________ (not/run) at all and he scores even more.

John: Oh, Gemma. ___________________ (you/know) the rules?

Gemma: Of course not. Girls _____________ (not/play) cricket at school.

John: So why did you go?

Gemma: Well, my brother bought the tickets and the picnic and I ____________ (love) picnics.

15 Ein Samstag zuhause. Streiche die falschen Verbformen durch.

It's Saturday morning and I sit/'m sitting in bed at home. I read/'m reading a book and I listen/'m listening to music. My parents have/are having breakfast downstairs. I can hear them. On Saturday I usually get up/am getting up early and go/am going jogging. Then I have/'m having breakfast and then I go/'m going to football training. I stay/'m staying at home today because I'm ill. And I like/'m liking it. I think I'll stay at home next week, too.

16 Jake und Ruth sind bei einem Skateboard-Turnier. Übersetze ins Englische.

Jake: Schau mal! Das Mädchen (da) macht grade einen tollen Trick.

____

Ruth: Ja, sie gewinnt oft.

____

Jake: Und was macht Jean im Moment?

____

Ruth: Sie wartet und hört Musik.

____

Jake: Warum schaut sie nicht zu?

____

Ruth: Sie schaut nie zu. Das macht sie nervös.

____

Wiederholung: Bestätigungsfragen

That's nice, **isn't it?** – Das ist schön, **nicht wahr?**

You don't like that, **do you?** – Du magst das nicht, **oder (doch)?**

Do you? und *isn't it?* sind ***question tags*** und können mit „oder?" oder „nicht wahr?" übersetzt werden.

Du bildest ein *question tag* mit einem Pronomen und dem Hilfsverb aus dem vorangehenden Satz. Wenn kein Hilfsverb vorhanden ist, nimmst du eine Form von *to do.*

Wenn der Aussagesatz negativ ist, ist das *question tag* positiv und umgekehrt.

positiver Aussagesatz	→ **negatives *question tag***
You play tennis, John's nice, They've been skiing,	don't you? isn't he? haven't they?
negativer Aussagesatz	→ **positives *question tag***
Those trousers aren't nice, You can't do that trick, Rob didn't win,	are they? can you? did he?

17 Beim Tennis. Verbinde die Aussagen mit der passenden Bestätigungsfrage.

You often go to the skateboard park,	is it?
You don't like the park in town,	can you?
That's your new skateboard,	do you?
That trick isn't easy,	don't you?
John has a new skateboard,	has he?
He's already won a competition on it,	doesn't he?
But he doesn't practise very often,	isn't it?
He hasn't taught you his new trick,	does he?
You can't do it already,	hasn't he?

18 Tom und Alice lernen sich beim Jugendklub kennen. Trage die richtigen Bestätigungsfragen ein.

Tom: You haven't been here before, ______________?

Alice: No, I haven't. And you know everybody here, ______________?

Tom: Yes, almost. I like it here. There are lots of things to do here, ______________?

Alice: Yes. Look! They're good at basketball, ______________?

Tom: Yes, they haven't made any silly mistakes, ______________?

Alice: No, they haven't. And you can play well, too, ______________?

Tom: Yes, but how do you know? Oh. You've just started at my school, ______________? And my friend, Mark, told you about this youth club, ______________?

Alice: Yes, he did. But he isn't here today, ______________?

Tom: No, he's ill. So we can play badminton together, ______________?

Tipp

Question tags sind im Englischen alltäglich. Sie beleben die Unterhaltung. Übe sie, indem du dir ein paar Aussagen auf Englisch überlegst und sie laut mit einem *question tag* sagst.

Zuhören: *question tags* 1

19 Höre dir den ersten Teil des Tracks an und notiere, welches *question tag* der Sprecher verwenden würde. Dann höre dir den zweiten Teil an und überprüfe, ob du recht hattest.

1. ______________ 3. ______________

2. ______________ 4. ______________

Das *present progressive* als Futur

Du kannst das ***present progressive*** auch verwenden, um über die Zukunft zu reden. Wenn du über **Vereinbarungen** sprichst, vor allem wenn schon **Zeit und Ort ausgemacht** sind, verwende das *present progressive:*

What **are** you **doing** at the weekend? – **I'm meeting** John in town on Saturday. We**'re going** to the cinema.

Das *present progressive* zur Wiedergabe der Zukunft ist dem *going to future* sehr ähnlich. In vielen Fällen können beide verwendet werden.

20 Ein sportliches Wochenende. Schau dir die Bilder und Wörter an und formuliere Sätze im *present progressive.*

weekend

What – you? ______________________________

____

I – Saturday

Pete – Sunday

____

we – watch

____

Zuhören: Gegenwart oder Zukunft? 2

21 Höre dir zunächst die Kurzdialoge auf der CD an. Dann entscheide dich: Beziehen sich die gesprochenen Sätze auf das *present* oder das *future?*

1. a) What are you doing? ____________
   b) I'm meeting Tina. ____________
2. He's playing tennis with some mates. ____________
3. a) Where are you going? ____________
   b) I'm going to the skatepark. ____________
   c) No, some friends are coming to my house at 8 pm. ____________

22 Gegenwart oder Zukunft? Lies den Text und vervollständige die Lücken mit dem *simple present* oder dem *present progressive.*

Tim: ____________ (you/go) to Brighton for the marathon tomorrow?

Mike: Yes, ____________ *(short answer)*. I ____________ (go) by bus. ____________ (you/want) to come with me?

Tim: I ____________ (not/know). I don't like marathons really. But I like the sea. What time ____________ (you/go)?

Mike: We ____________ (leave) about 12.30.

Tim: That's very early.

Mike: Yes, but I ____________ (meet) Pete at one so we can warm up first.

Tim: Why ____________ (you/want) to warm up first?

Mike: Didn't you know? We ____________ (run) in the marathon.

Sports

23 Lies die Beschreibungen der Sportarten einmal durch. Welcher Sport wird jeweils beschrieben?

1. This is a very old game but usually only people in English-speaking countries play it. When you go to English villages in the summer, you often see some people, usually men, who are playing the game on the village green, which is an area of grass in the middle of the village. There are eleven players on each team and the men usually wear white. They play the game with bats and a ball and it is quite a slow game. It is a game which is difficult to understand and it often looks like nothing is happening.

→ ______________________

2. Usually just two players play this sport, or one team with two players plays against another team. You play the game with a racket and a ball usually on a grass or a sand court. An umpire makes sure that everybody plays correctly.
People believe that this game also started in England and in Wales in the nineteenth century. The world's first club started in Leamington Spa near Birmingham in 1872. But before this time people played an older version of the game in France as early as the sixteenth century.

→ ______________________

3. We know that this game is over 4000 years old and that people have played it all over the world because we have found very old pictures from Africa, China and Greece, for example. But people think that the modern game started in England in the early nineteenth century.
Two teams have eleven players and must try to score goals with long sticks You usually play the game outside on a grass pitch but you can also play it inside. There are also other games that are almost the same. For example, there are versions of this game that you play on skates.

→ ______________________

Tipp

Wenn du einen Text liest, ist es nicht wichtig, gleich jedes einzelne Wort zu verstehen oder nachzuschlagen. Übe stattdessen, einen Text, egal wie schwer er dir vorkommt, erst einmal durchzulesen und die Wörter, die du nicht kennst, zu ignorieren. Beschäftige dich mit den Einzelheiten erst beim zweiten Lesen!

Informationen heraussuchen

24 Die Fragen beziehen sich auf den Text in Aufgabe 23. Versuche sie zu beantworten, möglichst ohne den Text noch einmal zu lesen.

Text 1:

1. How many players are there on each team? ____________________
2. What colour do they usually wear? ____________________
3. In which countries do they play this sport? ____________________

Text 2:

4. What do you need to play this game? ____________________
5. Where did this game start? ____________________

Text 3:

6. How old is this sport? ____________________
7. Where do you play this game? ____________________

Detailverständnis

25 Korrigiere die falschen Sätze.

Text 1: This game is very fast but it isn't hard to understand.

____

Text 2: People played a kind of this game later in France.

____

Text 3: Only people in England play this game.

____

Zuhören: ein Interview 3

26 Höre dir das Interview an und vervollständige danach das Profil.

_______: David Michael Roberts
Age: __________
Height: __________________
Weight: _________________
Birthday: ________________
Likes: ______________, __________________
Doesn't like: __________, __________________

Zuhören: *sounds* 4

27 Höre dir den CD-Track an und lies die Wörter durch. Dann unterstreiche die Wörter, die den angegebenen Laut beinhalten.

[g] rugby – traffic lights – age – fog

[k] kick – score – century – become

[l] foul – tackle – complain – talk

[s] shell – goggles – stone – sound

[t] net – tiring – chat – thank

Tipp Wenn du neue Wörter lernst, sage sie dir immer auch laut vor. Im Englischen sehen die Wörter meist anders aus, als sie sich anhören.

Zuhören: Fußball für Mädchen? 5

28 Höre dir die Diskussion über Fußball an, dann beantworte die Fragen.

1. Welche dieser Zusammenfassungen passt am besten zu der Diskussion?
a) Ann and Sally are trying to decide which sport is best; hockey or football. They decide that football is the best sport.
b) Ann wants to play football at school and thinks it isn't fair that girls can't play. Sally agrees with her and they decide to start a football team.
c) Ann likes football much better than hockey and thinks it isn't fair that girls can't play football at their school. Sally disagrees.

→ ______ passt am besten.

2. Verbinde die Sätze so, wie sie im gesprochenen Text vorkommen.

But, Ann, no other girls want to play football.	Oh, don't be silly.
Football's hard and dangerous – just like boys.	Yes, you're right.
That's the only way the other players can stop you.	Rubbish.
… football's just so much more fun than hockey.	That's not true.
They haven't got the skill.	Yes, I agree with you.

3. Sind diese Aussagen *true* oder *false?* Korrigiere die falschen Aussagen.

a) Ann thinks that football is more dangerous than hockey. ________

b) Ann thinks that many girls aren't very good with a hockey stick. ________

c) Sally likes to watch football. ________

d) Both girls think that women are better than men at football. ________

e) Ann has the idea to start a football team. ________

Korrektur: ____

____

Skills workshop 1

Eine Präsentation erarbeiten

Schritt 1: Entscheide dich für ein Thema.

Schritt 2: Sammle Ideen und Informationen. Trage zunächst alles zusammen und überlege später, was du davon verwenden willst. Nicht jede Einzelheit ist wichtig!

Schritt 3: Bereite die Informationen auf. Du kannst sie gruppieren, also in sinnvollen Einheiten zusammenfassen und in eine Reihenfolge bringen. Mach dir für deinen Vortrag Notizen auf Kärtchen. Nummeriere sie, damit du nicht durcheinanderkommst.

Schritt 4: Übe deine Präsentation. Trage sie jemandem vor oder übe sie vor dem Spiegel. Verwende eine Stoppuhr.

1 Sieh dir die Sätze an und trage ein, welcher Kategorie sie sich zuordnen lassen: **A** History of sport – **B** Early football – **C** The first rules

1. People first played sport when they didn't have to hunt all the time. ________
2. Pupils and the head teachers wrote some rules. ________
3. Football clubs started at expensive schools. ________
4. After 1800 workers didn't have time to play; they had to work more. ________
5. There were no rules at first for football. ________
6. Lots of people were on each team. ________
7. Kings didn't want so many people to play; they wanted them to fight. ________
8. First people ran and threw things and later they used balls. ________
9. People kicked, threw and carried the football. ________

2 Ordne jeweils zwei Sätze und Wendungen ihrer Verwendungsart zu, indem du sie mit einer Linie verbindest.

1. I'm not sure but I think …
2. We're going to tell you …
3. Are there any questions?
4. Sorry, but I don't know.
5. Thank you for listening.
6. As you can see in the picture …
7. Can you explain why …?
8. First I'd like to tell you …
9. Next …
10. Do you know who …?

start of talk

middle of talk

end of talk

asking questions

(not) answering questions

Zuhören: eine Präsentation verfolgen 6

3 Jetzt höre dir die Präsentation an. Welche der Sätze aus Aufgabe 2 werden verwendet?

Phrases: ____________________

4 Wie könntest du auf die Präsentation reagieren? Vervollständige die Sätze.

1. That was inter ______________.
2. I under ______________ every ______________.
3. You spoke very cl______________.
4. I really enj______________ that.

Test practice A

The football team

A "What are you doing, Ann?" asks Christine.
"I'm hanging up posters for our new girls' football team."
"Girls' football team? But girls don't play football."
"Rubbish! Of course, girls play football. They just don't play football at our school. That's why we're starting a football team – so that girls can play football. Don't you want to come?"
"No, you know I don't like sport," answers Christine.
Christine walks on and Ann puts some more posters on the walls. She wonders if she's making a mistake. Not many girls seem to be interested. She can't understand why. There's women's football at the Olympics and football isn't harder or more dangerous than lots of other women's sports. Hockey is harder and skateboarding is more dangerous, she thinks.

B On Wednesday Ann is walking home from school when she sees Sally.
"Hi Sally! Where are you going? Do you want to come back to our house and we can work on our History project?"
"No, I can't. I'm meeting my mum in town. I need to buy some clothes. What are you doing tomorrow?"
"I'm going to football training."
"Football training? But you haven't found enough girls yet, have you?"
"No, I haven't. So we're training with the boys tomorrow."
"With the boys? Wow. Oh, maybe I will come."
"Sally! Can't you think of anything else?" asks Ann and then says goodbye.

C It's three o'clock on Thursday and Ann's sitting in the Science lesson. She can't think well at all because she's so excited about the football training. Excited and nervous! The boys won't want to practise with us, she thinks, and maybe it will be terrible.
She goes to the football training and sees three other girls she knows and then she sees Sally. Sally is wearing new training shoes and new sports clothes and talking to all the boys.
"Sally, what are you doing here?" asks Ann.
"Oh, I saw these clothes yesterday in town and I just had to wear them today," she says and laughs.
"Hey, we're not here to talk. We're here to play football," says the teacher when he arrives. "You haven't even warmed up yet. Come on. Five times round the pitch. Let's see who's fastest?"

They all run. The boys run fast but Ann is fast, too. She wants to win the race, but she isn't quite fast enough. She's almost finished when she hears the boys' voices. They are all cheering for Sally. Sally is running slowly around the field – she's jogging and smiling. She isn't even tired. Ann isn't happy about it – she thinks Sally's turning the training into a joke.

D After that they practise with the balls in groups. The girls practise together. They kick the ball to each other and Ann is surprised; all the girls can kick the ball really well. She really enjoys it. Then they play two on three. Before they go, they practise at the goal. Ann's tired but she has really enjoyed herself. Now she really wants to kick well and score lots of goals so that the boys see that they can play well and so that they can train with them again. When it's her turn, she runs at the ball, kicks and misses the goal completely. Nobody laughs; the boys are all quite friendly but she's not happy. Then it's Sally's turn. She acts the clown again and everybody laughs. She should be an actress, thinks Ann. But then, when she kicks the ball, she kicks it so hard that it flies into the net, between the goalkeeper's legs. Everybody cheers.
"Where did you learn to do that?" asks Ann later.
"Oh, I always played with my brothers and their friends at home," says Sally, "but you know, I think hockey is more fun."

Reading

1 Welche Absätze passen am besten zu den folgenden Überschriften?

1. The girls play well. ________________
2. It's often difficult to start something new. ________________
3. A surprise player. ________________
4. No time for homework. ________________

2 Auf wen passen die folgenden Beschreibungen?

1. She enjoys sport and football best. ________________
2. She doesn't like sport at all. ________________
3. She has played football with her brother. ________________

3 Welche Antwort passt? Kreuze an.

1. Ann thinks that girls ... a) don't like football ☐, b) can't play football ☐, c) want to play football ☐.

2. Ann thinks skateboarding ... a) is more dangerous ☐, b) is harder ☐, c) is more fun ☐.

3. On Wednesday Sally ... a) does her homework ☐, b) meets her mum ☐, c) goes to football training ☐.

4. Sally says she's at training ... a) to wear her new clothes ☐, b) to play football ☐, c) to help her friend Ann ☐.

5. The boys cheer because ... a) Sally runs so fast ☐, b) Ann runs so fast ☐, c) Sally runs so slowly and smiles ☐.

6. Sally can ... a) score great goals ☐, b) throw the ball well ☐, c) tackle well ☐.

Language

4 Beziehen sich diese Sätze aus dem Text auf *past*, *present* oder *future?*

1. What are you doing, Ann? (line 1) ______________
2. I'm going to football training. (line 17) ______________
3. But you haven't found enough girls yet ... (line 18) ______________
4. The boys won't want to practise with us ... (line 25) ______________
5. She thinks Sally's turning the training into a joke. (line 34) ______________
6. Where did you learn to do that? (line 48) ______________

Passing on information

5 Deine englische Cousine möchte etwas vom Kapitän des Fußballteams wissen. Hilf ihr, indem du für die beiden dolmetschst.

Cousin: When are you practising next?

You: ______________________________

Captain: Wir trainieren am Freitagnachmittag. Möchtest du mit uns spielen?

You: ______________________________

Cousin: Yes, please. See you on Friday.

You: ______________________________

Listening 7

6 Höre dir die Unterhaltung auf der CD an und notiere: Wann, wo und wozu verabreden sich die beiden Mädchen?

When: ____________ Where: ____________ What: ____________

Writing

7 Schau dir die Stichpunkte an und schreibe drei oder vier Sätze über Ann.

Full name: Ann Jane Ellis
Age: 14
Likes: all sport, hip hop music
Doesn't like: rice, History homework

____

____

____

Unit 2

London

1 Sieh dir die Bilder an und beschrifte sie.

1. ______________ 2. ______________ 3. ______________ 4. ______________

2 Unterwegs in London. Ergänze die Lücken mit den richtigen Wörtern.

building – Ferris wheel – landmarks – paintings – parade – royal family

Last weekend I went on my first trip to London. Of course, I wanted to see all the famous ______________ so I went to Buckingham Palace first. I hoped to see the ______________ there but I think they were on holiday at one of their palaces in Scotland. I went on a tour of the ______________ anyway and it was interesting to see all the old and expensive ______________ on the wall. Then I went on the London Eye which is a big ______________ on the River Thames. You get a great view from there. But the very best part of my trip came at the end. We went to the Notting Hill Carnival and watched the ______________ there. We ate delicious food and danced in the streets. Yes, it was brilliant.

Orte

3 Finde sechs Orte in der Wortschlange und schreibe sie neben die richtige Erklärung.

1. You may stay here when you go on holiday. ______________________
2. If you want to learn more when you are older, go here. ______________________
3. Kings and queens live in one of these. ______________________
4. This place is like a big church. ______________________
5. You can buy fruit and vegetables here. ______________________
6. You can watch plays here. ______________________

Unterwegs mit der *Tube*

4 Verbinde die Satzhälften zu sinnvollen ganzen Sätzen.

Could you	the Central Line westbound.
How do I	off at Covent Garden.
Take	get to Covent Garden Market, please?
Change at	Holborn after three stops.
Change	help me, please?
Get	to the Piccadilly Line southbound.

Tipp Lerne ganze Sätze oder Wendungen auswendig. Spreche sie dir laut vor, bis sie natürlich klingen.

Berufe

5 Sieh dir die Bilder an. Welche Berufe haben die dargestellten Personen?

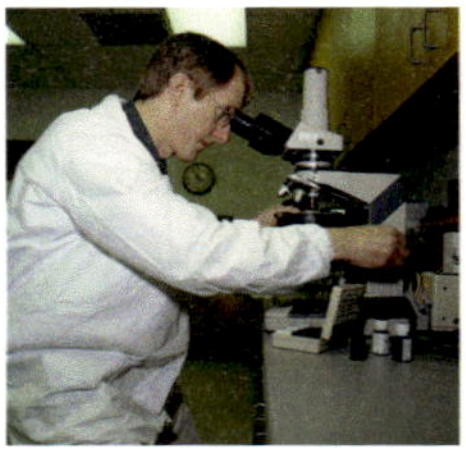

1. ____________________ 2. ____________________ 3. ____________________

4. ____________________ 5. ____________________ 6. ____________________

6 Ergänze das Wortgitter und stelle aus den hinterlegten Kästchen die Lösungsworte zusammen.

1. They're not 20 yet.
2. Your sister's son.
3. He or she designs houses.
4. This person lives next door.
5. He or she gets money when somebody dies.
6. A helper.
7. This person takes from a bag or a coat.

Girls put their _ _ y _, mobile and purse in it: _ _ _ d _ _ _

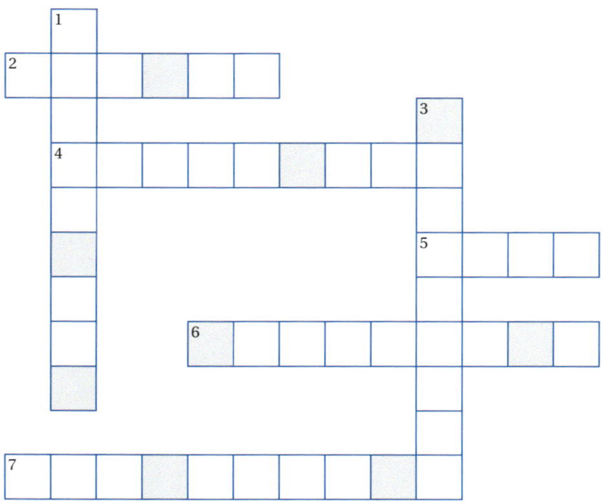

Kleidung und Accessoires

7 Beschrifte die beiden Bilder.

1. ____________________
2. ____________________
3. ____________________

4. ____________________
5. ____________________

6. ____________________
7. ____________________
8. ____________________

9. ____________________
10. ____________________
11. ____________________

Menschen beschreiben

8 Löse die Anagramme auf und trage die Wörter in passenden Lücken ein.

onelly – godo-kogloin – manorl – afir

1. Her hair isn't dark. It's ____________________.
2. She's beautiful, isn't she? Yes, she's very ____________________.
3. He's not very clever or very strong. He's just ____________________.
4. He lives on his own. He's a bit ____________________.

Verben

9 Suche elf Wörter aus dem Wortgitter heraus und ordne sie ihren Übersetzungen zu.

hinzufügen: ______________

sich streiten: ______________

fertigstellen: ______________

entwerfen: ______________

fallen lassen: ______________

springen: ______________

hochheben: ______________

d	r	o	p	c	a	z	j
b	m	s	h	o	o	t	k
r	u	p	r	m	f	s	l
o	j	u	m	p	d	s	i
b	s	s	a	l	e	n	f
a	f	h	k	e	s	i	t
y	w	t	j	t	i	f	a
a	r	g	u	e	g	f	i
a	d	d	x	f	n	h	v

schieben: ______________ schießen: ______________

ausrauben: ______________ schnüffeln: ______________

10 Sherlock Holmes! Trage die Verben richtig ein und denke dabei an die korrekte Zeitform.

A famous man with lots of money m a _ _ _ _ _ a woman and then somebody m _ r _ _ _ _ _ him. Everybody thinks his wife k _ _ _ _ _ him. She needs help. Who can s _ _ v _ the mystery? Sherlock Holmes. He n _ _ i _ _ _ everything. He asks the wife and the servants questions and they d _ _ _ _ _ b _ what they saw and what happened. He calls the police and they a r _ _ _ _ a servant. How did he know who did it? "Elementary, my dear Watson," he says.

Wiederholung: der *s*-Genitiv

Man verwendet den **s-Genitiv,** um einen Besitz auszudrücken:

There is the girl'**s** brother.	... der Bruder des Mädchens.
Where's the dog'**s** ball?	... der Ball des Hundes?
A man stole the boy**s'** bikes.	... die Fahrräder der Jungen.
The cousin**s'** dads are brothers.	Die Väter der Cousinen ...

Wenn die Besitzer in der **Mehrzahl** sind, kommt der **Apostroph nach dem** ***s*:** boy**s'**, cousin**s'**. So unterscheidet man zwischen *one boy's bags* und *two boys' bags*.
Wenn eine unregelmäßige Mehrzahlform verwendet wird, wenn es also kein Plural-*s* gibt, z. B. bei *women* oder *people*, verwendet man **'s,** um Missverständnisse zu vermeiden:

The women'**s** childen were at school (die Kinder der Frauen).
People'**s** rubbish was everywhere (der Müll der Menschen).

11 Ein Verbrechen in London. Übersetze die Sätze.

1. Sir Elliot's children's dog always sniffed at their visitors.

____

2. Sir Elliot's servant looked after his heirs' dogs.

____

3. The servants' rooms are in the main house's attic.

____

4. The family's friend was Sherlock Holmes.

____

5. The Elliots' neighbour killed their daughters' dog.

____

Wiederholung: die einfache Vergangenheit

Du verwendest das ***simple past***, um zu sagen, was passiert und bereits vorbei ist:

Yesterday I **went** to London. (Ich war dort und bin wieder hier.)

Bei Vollverben verwendest du *did*, um Fragen und Verneinungen zu bilden. Die Form ist bei jeder Person gleich:

Where **did** you **go** yesterday?	Wo bist du gestern gewesen?
I **visited** the Queen.	Ich besuchte die Königin.
Did you **enjoy** it? – **Yes, I did.**	Hat's dir gefallen? – Ja.
My sisters **didn't come.**	Meine Schwestern kamen nicht.

Wenn du eine Frage mit *to be* bilden willst, stellst du *was* oder *were* vor das Subjekt:

Where **were** you at nine? You **weren't** at home. – I **was** at my neighbours' party. – **Was** it good? – Yes, it **was.**

Signalwörter: yesterday, … ago, last week/month/Wednesday

12 Ein Besuch in London. Ergänze in dem Dialog die richtigen Verbformen.

John: ______________________ (you/have) a good time in London?

Karen: Yes, I _______________ (go) to Camden Market.

John: ______________________ (you/buy) lots of clothes?

Karen: Yes, _______________ *(short answer)*, and in the afternoon I _______________ (meet) lots of famous people.

John: Who ______________________ (you/meet)?

Karen: I _______________ (meet) the Queen and Paul McCartney.

John: Oh, what ______________________ (they/say)?

Karen: Oh, they ______________________ (not/speak). They _______________ (not/be) real. I _______________ (see) them at Madame Tussauds, the famous wax *(Wachs)* museum.

Wiederholung: das Perfekt

Mit dem ***present perfect*** drückst du aus, dass eine Handlung in der Vergangenheit *(perfect)* mit der Gegenwart *(present)* in Verbindung steht.

Zum Beispiel kann die Folge der Handlung spürbar sein:

I'**ve broken** my arm. (I broke it yesterday and it still hurts now.)
She'**s never been** to London. (She doesn't know what it's like now.)

Oder etwas fing in der Vergangenheit an und gilt immer noch:

John **has lived** here **for** two years. (He moved here two years ago and still lives here.)

Oder eine Handlung ist gerade abgeschlossen:

We'**ve just eaten.**

Man bildet das Perfekt mit *have/has* und dem *past participle:*

They **haven't eaten** yet.
Have you **eaten?** – Yes, I **have.**

Signalwörter: already, just, never, ever, (not) … yet, for … years/days

13 Bilde korrekte Sätze mit dem Perfekt.

you – visit – London – before – ?

____

no *(short answer)* / I – not – be – here before

____

my brother – live – here – for three years

____

what – he – do – here – ?

____

he – learn – English – and – meet – lots of – nice people

____

Wiederholung: das Perfekt und die einfache Form der Vergangenheit

Du verwendest das ***simple past,*** wenn du sagen möchtest, **wann** etwas passiert ist:

I **broke** my arm **yesterday.** → Der Zeitpunkt ist wichtig.

Du verwendest das ***present perfect,*** wenn das **Ergebnis** wichtig ist, nicht der Zeitpunkt:

I**'ve broken** my arm. → Der Arm ist noch gebrochen.

Auch der Zeitpunkt der Aussage oder Frage spielt eine Rolle:

Have you **eaten** this morning? → Hier verwendest du das *present perfect,* weil es noch morgens ist.

Did you **eat** this morning? → Hier verwendest du das *simple past,* weil es schon abends ist.

Oft wird das *present perfect* verwendet, um zu sagen, dass etwas passiert ist, und dann das *simple past,* um weitere Einzelheiten mitzuteilen:

Have you **ever been** to Italy? **Did** you **like** it there?

Signalwörter: *present perfect:* never, ever, so far, already, yet, just; *simple past:* yesterday, in 2003, … ago, when, last …

14 *Present perfect* oder *simple past?* Bilde vollständige Sätze.

I – already – to see – three museums

____

John – to visit – Buckingham Palace – yesterday

____

you – ever – to meet – the Queen – ?

____

what – you – to do – last week – ?

____

15 Sue übernachtet bei ihrer Cousine in London und ruft von dort aus ihre Mutter an. Unterstreiche die richtigen Verbformen.

Mum: Have you done/Did you do anything exciting yet?

Sue: Yes, I have/did. I have already been/was already on the London Eye. And yesterday I've been/went to Camden Market.

Mum: Oh, I've never been/never went there. Has it been/Was it nice?

Sue: Yes, it has/was. I have bought/bought a leather handbag there. But somebody has already stolen/already stole it.

Mum: Oh no. When has that happened/did that happen?

Sue: Last night when I have been/went to the Notting Hill Carnival. But don't worry. The police have just called/just called. They have already found it.

16 Der Notting Hill Carnival. Vervollständige die Übersetzung.

Der Notting Hill Carnival fand zum ersten Mal 1964 statt.

______________________________ for the first time in 1964.

Die Menschen gehen seit 20 Jahren gern dorthin *(enjoy).*

____________________________________ for 20 years.

Gestern Abend habe ich auf der Straße getanzt.

____

Ich habe noch nie ein so interessantes Essen gegessen.

________________________________ such interesting food.

Die Verlaufsform der Vergangenheit

Du verwendest das ***past progressive,*** um zu sagen, was an einem bestimmten Punkt in der Vergangenheit passiert ist und noch nicht abgeschlossen ist. Die Handlung verläuft also noch.

Du bildest das *past progressive* mit *was/were* + Verb + Endung *-ing*.

Aussagen:

I **was sleeping** at 9. They **were dancing.**

Verneinungen:

She **wasn't watching** TV at 12. They **weren't eating.**

Fragen:

What **were** you **doing** at seven o'clock? – I **was helping** my mum.

Were you **cleaning** the house? – Yes, I **was.**

17 Um Mitternacht. Trage die richtige Formen der Verben ein.

What ______________________ (you/do) at 12 o'clock last night?

I ______________________ (read) a scary book.

My brothers ______________________ (look for) monsters under the bed.

And ______________________ (your dad/watching) TV?

No, ______________ *(short answer)*. My dad ______________________ (work).

My older sister ______________________ (dance) in a disco.

We ______________________ (not/sleep) but we didn't hear the thieves. They ______________________ (drive) our car away.

18 Schau dir die Bilder genau an. Dann formuliere Fragen, Kurzantworten und wenn nötig die richtige Antwort im *past progressive*.

Was ______________________________ (buy something)?

– ____________________ *(short answer).*

He ____.

____ (listen to music)? – ____________________ *(short answer).*

____ (eat chips)? – ____________________ *(short answer).* They

____.

____?

(visit London) – ____________________ *(short answer).*

____

______________________________ (plan their trip).

19 In der *Tube.* Übersetze mit dem *past progressive.*
Was hast du gestern um 18 Uhr im U-Bahnhof gemacht? – Ich wartete auf einen Zug. Ein Mann stahl meinen Geldbeutel. Aber die Polizei hat es beobachtet.

____

____

____

Die Verlaufsform und die einfache Form der Vergangenheit

Wenn du über eine abgeschlossene Handlung in der Vergangenheit oder über eine Reihe von Handlungen redest, verwendest du das ***simple past:***

Yesterday I **went** to town. First I **bought** some clothes, then I **met** some friends and then we **had** lunch.

Wenn du ausdrücken möchtest, dass eine Handlung zu einem bestimmten Zeitpunkt in der Vergangenheit länger andauerte, verwendest du das ***past progressive:***

I **was eating** lunch yesterday at 12 o'clock. → Ich fing vor 12 an zu essen und aß nach 12 noch immer.

Oft verwendet man das ***simple past*** und das ***past progressive*** zusammen, um zu sagen, dass während des Verlaufs einer Handlung eine neue anfing:

I **was watching** TV when a friend **called.** – Ich sah (schon länger) fern, als (plötzlich mittenhinein) ein Freund anrief.

While we **were waiting** for a train, we **met** a friend. – Als wir auf einen Zug warteten, begegneten wir einem Freund.

Im ***while***-Satz steht ***past progressive,*** im ***when***-Satz steht ***simple past.***

20 Ein Besuch in Buckingham Palace. Verbinde die Satzteile sinnvoll miteinander.

I was walking through London	while I was sitting in a living room.
While I was taking a photo,	I was sitting at my desk at home.
She was walking in the garden	William was swimming in it.
She showed me her house	while we were waiting for the tea.
When I saw the swimming pool,	when I saw Buckingham Palace.
I fell asleep	when she invited me for a cup of tea.
When I woke up,	the Queen arrived.

Zuhören und nachdenken 8

21 In Hyde Park. Höre dir den CD-Track an und beschreibe mit den angegebenen Wörtern, was passiert ist. Verwende je nachdem *when* oder *while*.

he – break his leg – they – play football – while

____

a woman – ride a horse – her mobile – ring – when

____

the man – listen to his radio – he – fall asleep – while

____

22 Noch einmal Glück gehabt. Trage die richtigen Formen der Verben ein.

I ________________ (travel) to Covent Garden on the Tube when I ________________ (meet) a friend. While we ________________ (talk), the train ________________ (stop) at Covent Garden. The doors ________________ (close) when my friend ________________ (say), “Didn’t you want to get off here?” I got off and the train ________________ (leave) when I ________________ (remember) that my bag was still on the train. My mobile phone, my money and my train ticket were in the bag. I was just thinking, “What can I do now?” when I ________________ (see) another friend. One phone call and ten minutes later I had my bag again.

Das Plusquamperfekt

Wenn du sagen möchtest, dass etwas vor etwas anderem in der Vergangenheit passiert ist, verwendest du das ***past perfect:***

When I arrived at the museum, it **had** already **closed.** ≈ The museum closed first and then I arrived there.

She was late for school because she **had missed** the bus. ≈ She missed the bus and then she was late for school.

Das *past perfect* wird mit *had* und dem *past participle* gebildet. Es ist für alle Personen gleich und wird oft zusammen mit dem *simple past* verwendet.

23 Im Theater. Formuliere die Sätze um, indem du das *past perfect* verwendest.

1. I heard the Globe Theatre was interesting and so I visited it.

→ I ________________ the Globe Theatre because I ________________ that it was interesting.

2. We visited the theatre and then we bought some tickets for a play.

→ We ________________ some tickets for a play after we ______________ ______________ the theatre.

3. I read the book by Shakespeare and then we saw the play.

→ When we ________________ the play, I __________ already __________ the book by Shakespeare.

4. The play started and then we arrived.

→ The play ________________ when we ________________ at the theatre.

5. I saw the play and then I wanted to become an actress.

→ After I ______________ the play, I ______________ to become an actress.

24 Was passiert auf den Bildern? Formuliere Sätze mit dem *past perfect*.

leave – get to

1. The bus ______________________________ when she ____________________ the bus stop.

2. The play ____________________________ before she ____________________________ at the theatre.

start – arrive

25 Aufregung am London Eye. Vervollständige die Lücken mit der richtigen Form des *simple past* oder *past perfect*.

I ______________________________ (already/eat) breakfast when Mary called and suggested that we go on the London Eye that day. When I __________ __________ (arrive) at the London Eye, there was a big queue. That didn't matter because I __________________________ (already/buy) tickets on the Internet. We ____________________________ (agree) to meet at 10 so I bought the tickets for 10.30. At 10.30 Mary had still not arrived so I __________ __________ (decide) to go on my own. I had already entered the capsule when I __________________ (see) Mary. I jumped out again and ran to Mary. We ____________________________ (just/enter) a second capsule when the London Eye broke down. Lots of people were in the air and couldn't get down. "Oh, I am glad you were late," I said.

Die Abenteuer von Shirley Holmes

26 Lies erst die Geschichte durch. Dann wähle die beste Überschrift aus.

A) Grandma catches a thief. ☐ C) When the milkman rings. ☐

B) Everybody loves Beethoven. ☐ D) Shirley catches a thief. ☐

Shirley Holmes had just arrived at her grandma's house.
"Would you like a cup of tea?" asked Grandma.
"Oh, yes please. And then you can tell me what has happened," said Shirley.
Grandma brought the cup of tea and then sat down.
"Well," said Grandma, "I think somebody is stealing from me."
"Oh no. What have they stolen?"
"I think they have stolen money and an expensive pen and a classical CD and ... but I'm not really sure. Maybe I have just lost the things."
"When did you ... er, lose them then?" asked Shirley.
"I don't know really. I just know that I cannot find my best pen. I'm sure it was here on the television a few days ago. And I think money has gone from my purse."
"Well, let's think," said Shirley. "Who could steal things from you? Who comes to your house?"
"The milkman comes."
"The milkman? Does he come in here?"
"Yes, sometimes he does. If he sees me, he brings the milk in the house and when I pay him, he comes in, too. But he's a very nice and friendly man."
"Hm. So he knows where your purse is," said Shirley to herself.
"Yes. And two of my neighbours, Jean and Doris, often come in for a cup of tea but I'm sure they don't steal anything. Kevin often comes in."
"Who's Kevin?"
"Oh, he lives around the corner and sometimes he comes in while he's waiting for his mum to get back from work."
"OK," said Shirley. "If it's OK with you, I'll stay here with you for a few days and see if I can find the thief."
"Oh yes, Shirley. That's very nice of you. Thanks," said Grandma.

Shirley stayed at her grandma's house and the very next day Kevin came round. Kevin was wearing new shoes.
"Those shoes are nice," said Shirley. "Are they new?"
"Yes, they are," he said, "I bought them yesterday with some money I had found."
"You found some money? That's very lucky. Where did you find it?"
"Oh, I found it last month in town and I took it to the police. Nobody came and said they'd lost the money so yesterday the police gave me the money

back again. And I went shopping right away."
Kevin stayed for a while and Grandma gave him some biscuits and he talked about school.
The next day Shirley was having breakfast when the milkman came. He was singing to himself and he seemed happy. Grandma was in the kitchen and called "Good morning" to him, so he brought the milk into the house for her. He didn't see Shirley who was in the living room. He talked to Grandma for a bit and while Grandma was putting the milk in the fridge *(Kühlschrank),* he looked round the kitchen.
"I like that music," he said. "What is it? Is it Mozart?"
"No, no," said Grandma. "It's Beethoven. It is very nice, isn't it?"
"Yes," said the milkman. "Well. Goodbye and have a nice day."

The next day the neighbours Jean and Doris came round. They both came together. They had a cup of tea and talked about all their neighbours. And then they talked about the milkman, too.
"He's a very nice man, isn't he?" said Doris.
"Yes, he is, and he's very helpful. He often brings the milk into my house," said Jean.
"And he loves music. He always listens to that Discman of his, doesn't he? And sings to himself."

"Please give me my purse back," said Shirley the next day as she walked into the kitchen.
"But I haven't got it," said the milkman.
Shirley had left her purse in the kitchen to trick the milkman. She had hidden under the table and then filmed him with her camcorder as he took it. Shirley showed him her camcorder. Then she called the police.
"But I thought he was such a nice man. How did you know that he was the thief?" asked Grandma.

27 Was hast du über die Charaktere erfahren? Kreuze an.

1. Shirley … drinks tea ☐, drinks milk ☐, lives near Grandma ☐.

2. Grandma … likes music ☐, drinks milk ☐, lives in a flat ☐.

3. Kevin … likes music ☐, drinks milk ☐, goes to school ☐.

4. The milkman … likes music ☐, drinks milk ☐, knows Jean and Doris ☐.

5. Jean … drinks tea ☐, drinks milk ☐, lives near Grandma ☐.

6. Doris … drinks tea ☐, drinks milk ☐, lives near Grandma ☐.

28 Wie kam Shirley darauf, wer der Dieb sein könnte, bevor sie ihn mit dem Camcorder filmte? Finde drei Sätze im Text, die darauf hinweisen.

1. ______________________________

2. ______________________________

3. ______________________________

29 Sieh dir das Bild zur Geschichte in Aufgabe 26 an. Was ist daran falsch? Finde die drei Fehler und notiere sie auf Englisch.

1. ______________________________
____

2. ______________________________
____

3. ______________________________
____

30 Beantworte die Fragen in einem oder mehreren Worten.

1. What happened after Shirley arrived at Grandma's? ______________
2. What does Kevin do in Grandma's house? ______________
3. What had Kevin just bought? ______________
4. What music was Grandma playing when the milkman came? ______________
5. What did Doris and Jean drink at Grandma's? ______________
6. What did the milkman steal at the end? ______________

Zuhören: Wortbetonung 9

31 Wie werden die Wörter betont? Trage die Wörter in der richtige Spalte ein. Höre dir dann den CD-Track an und überprüfe deine Antworten.

colourful – detective – market – normal – parade – skeleton – within – cathedral

Xx	xX	Xxx	xXx
______	______	______	______
______	______	______	______

Tipp Wenn du neue Wörter lernst, sprich sie laut aus, damit du auch gleich die richtige Betonung parat hast.

Zuhören: im Tower of London 10

32 Höre dir die CD an, dann stelle die Sätze in die richtige Reihenfolge, indem du sie nummerierst.

_____ Calvin went to the toilet.

_____ He saw a ghost.

_____ He sat down and had a drink and a sandwich.

_____ Calvin's class went down to the dungeons.

_____ Calvin looked in some dungeons and found a door.

_____ The dungeon door closed.

_____ The ghost showed him the way out.

_____ His teacher found him.

Zuhören: ein Ausflug nach London 11

33 Mary und ihre Freunde sprechen über ihre Pläne fürs Wochenende. Du hörst zuerst ihre Diskussion *(part 1)*, dann Mary an einer Kasse *(part 2)*. Ordne die Sätze unten richtig zu: Werden sie in *part 1* oder *2* gesprochen? Dann höre die CD noch einmal an und prüfe, ob du recht hattest.

Excuse me. ____________

Well, how about a trip to London? ____________

And where can I get a brochure, please? ____________

Can we take photos in the theatre? ____________

How much are the tickets, please? ____________

And why don't we check what's on at the theatre, too? ____________

We could go to the Science Museum. ____________

That's a good idea. ____________

… how should we get there? ____________

We'd like to see Romeo and Juliet this afternoon, please. ____________

Shall I get a timetable? ____________

Are there special prices for children? ____________

34 Noch einmal CD 11: Welche Aussage ist richtig? Unterstreiche.

They want to go to London by bus/tram/train.

They want to buy some tickets for the train/theatre on the Internet.

They buy three/five tickets which cost five/33 pounds at the theatre.

They needn't/mustn't take photos in the theatre.

Skills workshop 2

Wörterbücher verwenden

In einem Wörterbuch sind die Wörter **alphabetisch** sortiert. Ein Eintrag beinhaltet auch Wortzusammensetzungen, Ableitungen und grammatikalische Informationen.
Oft haben deutsche Wörter auf Englisch mehrere Bedeutungen und umgekehrt. Wenn du also ein englisches Wort nachschlägst, solltest du erst **alle Bedeutungen durchlesen** und dann diejenige auswählen, die am besten in den **Zusammenhang** passt.
Auch wenn du die **Übersetzung** für ein englisches Wort suchst, solltest du **den ganzen Eintrag durchlesen** und nicht das erstbeste Wort nehmen. Hier helfen dir **Beispiele,** wie ein Wort verwendet wird. Auch eine **Rücküberprüfung** im jeweils anderen Wörterbuchteil kann dir zeigen, ob du richtig liegst.
Im englischen Teil ist in **Lautschrift** angegeben, wie ein Wort ausgesprochen wird, z. B. *tomb raider:* [tuːm ˈreɪdəʳ]. Außerdem sind **nützliche Ausdrücke** und **Redewendungen** enthalten, die oft eine ganz andere Bedeutung haben als die wortwörtliche. So bedeutet z. B. *Are you pulling my leg?* nicht „Ziehst du an meinem Bein?“ sondern „Willst du mich auf den Arm nehmen?“

1 Übersetze mithilfe eines Wörterbuches die hervorgehobenen Wörter.

1. Would you like a date? They're so sweet. ____________________
2. What date is it today? ____________________
3. I'd like to date John. He's very nice. ____________________
4. We're going to move to London tomorrow. ____________________
5. Can you move, please? You're standing on my foot. ____________________
6. I'm going to change. I'm all wet. ____________________
7. Have you got any change, please? For the phone. ____________________

2 Verwende ein Wörterbuch, um das jeweils richtige englische Wort auszuwählen.

1. Es ist niemand zu Hause. – Hast du die richtige Nummer gewählt?

a) to choose b) to dial c) to vote

2. Wo ist meine Uhr? Sie ist nicht in meiner Tasche.

a) clock b) o'clock c) watch

3. Ich habe einen tollen Preis in einem Wettbewerb gewonnen.

a) praise b) price c) prize

4. Meine Kinder sind jetzt alle groß. Sie wohnen nicht mehr zu Hause.

a) grown up b) big c) tall

3 Kannst du die Lautschrift lesen? Finde heraus, was die Sätze bedeuten.

1. [ˈevrɪbɒdɪ kæn biː ə dɪˈtektɪv]

____

2. [ðə ˈsɜːvənt wɒz ðə ˈmɜːdərəʳ]

____

4 Finde mithilfe eines Wörterbuchs heraus, was die folgenden Wendungen bedeuten.

1. Since I met her I've been on cloud nine.

____

2. I've read that but it's all Greek to me.

____

Revision A (Unit 1–2)

Menschen und Dinge

1 Löse das Kreuzworträtsel und versuche, anhand der hinterlegten Felder das Lösungswort herauszufinden.

1. He stops goals.
2. Hair on man's face.
3. The referee in a tennis game.
4. You wear these over your eyes.
5. Your sister's son.
6. He or she can do great tricks on a board.
7. He or she can help you.
8. You wear this on your foot.
9. A shoe for your hand.
10. He or she can solve mysteries.
11. A cook.
12. You use this to play tennis.

You don't want to meet this person: ______________________

Verben mit Objekt

2 Ordne die Verben einem passenden Objekt zu.

change **design** **marry** **notice** **score**

shoot **smoke** **solve**

to ____________ a pipe ____________ a woman

____________ a clue ____________ gun

____________ a building ____________ one's mind

____________ a mystery ____________ a goal

Unregelmäßige Verben

3 Vervollständige die Tabelle.

infinitive	*simple past*	*past participle*	*German*
			anfangen
		become	
	broke		
to catch			
	felt		
		hit	
			zittern
		shot	

Das Plusquamperfekt

4 Ein Skateboard-Turnier. Formuliere mithilfe der Satzteile ganze Sätze.

1. I learnt some tricks – then I saw the poster

→ When I ______________ the poster, I _________________ some new tricks.

2. The competition started – I arrived

→ The competition ______________________ when I ____________________.

3. I practised for two minutes – I broke my board

→ I _________________ for two minutes when I ________________ my board.

4. I borrowed a skateboard – I won the competition

→ After I _________________ a skateboard, I _____________ the competition.

Gegenwart oder Zukunft?

5 Verbinde die Satzteile, um einen sinnvollen Dialog zu erstellen, und schreibe sie auf.

What do you usually	play tennis with my dad.
I usually	are watching a match at Wimbledon.
What are you	is playing tomorrow?
We aren't	an umpire there.
We	playing tennis.
My dad knows	do on Saturdays?
He	going to play in the final.
Who	is talking to his friend now.
My favourite star is	doing tomorrow?

Die Verlaufsform der Vergangenheit

6 Im Bus. Formuliere Sätze mit den angegebenen Wörtern.

I – run – along the street – when – I – see – the bus

____

I – sit – on the bus – when – the bus – break down

____

Alle Zeitformen

7 Schreibe die Verben in der richtigen Zeit in den Lücken.

My dreams ____________________ (come true); I've met a girl who likes me, too. I saw her first while a boy _______________ (rob) her in London. She __________________ (wait) at a bus stop when he ____________ (push) her and she dropped her rucksack. I ______________________ (just/get off) a bus and I helped her to pick her things up and call the police. She thanked me and we ______________ (chat) to each other for an hour. We didn't even notice that it __________________ (start) to rain. How can I describe her? Well, she's funny and she's good at sport. When we _____________ (play) tennis, she can hit the ball hard. She ____________ (make) me laugh and I always ______________ (feel) happy when she's there. I _______________ (meet) her tomorrow. We _______________ (go) to London again. And will we marry? I don't know. But if things go wrong, it _____________________ (not/matter), she's got a nice friend, too.

Kommunikationsübung

8 Du übernachtest mit deinen Eltern in einem B & B in London. Ihr überlegt, was ihr unternehmen wollt. Deine Eltern möchten die Wirtin fragen, aber da sie nicht besonders gut Englisch sprechen, musst du vermitteln.

Mutter: Frag sie bitte, was wir nicht verpassen sollten.

Du: ______________________________

Wirtin: Well, why don't you go on the London Eye? The view is great.

Du: ______________________________

Vater: Das ist eine gute Idee. Wie kommen wir dahin?

Du: ______________________________

Wirtin: Well, you can take the Central Line to Bank. That's westbound. Then change at Bank to the Northern Line. Get off at London Bridge. That's the first stop and you can walk from there.

Du: ______________________________

____

____

Mutter: Danke sehr! Frag sie noch, ob der Buckingham Palace auch in der Nähe ist.

Du: ______________________________

Wirtin: It isn't very far. You can walk there or you can take the Jubilee Line northbound to Green Park. That's only two stops.

Du: ______________________________

____

Vater: Thanks very much.

Hörverstehen: Wer hat gewonnen? 12

9 Höre dir die CD an, dann stelle die Sätze mithilfe von Ziffern in die richtige Reihenfolge.

_______ Mike's team scored a goal in the right goal.

_______ The other team scored a goal in the right goal.

_______ The other team scored a goal in the wrong goal.

_______ They noticed that the referee's clock had stopped.

_______ They argued about who had won.

Schreiben: Tennisstars

10 Schreibe mithilfe der Notizen einen zusammenhängenden Text. Verwende das Plusquamperfekt, wo möglich.

Venus and Serena Williams – sisters. Their father – teach – them – to play tennis. Their father – learn – about tennis from a video.
The Williams' family – grow up – in Los Angeles – and – they – not have – much money. Their father – want – them – to do well – at sport – so that – they – can – have – a better life. They – work hard – and – they already – win – lots of matches – before – they – even – 14 years old.

Unit 3

A poetry slam

1 Ergänze den Text mit den angegebenen Wörtern.

argument – girlfriend – performance – poet – poetry – respect – response

Have you got something to say? Well, we've got people who want to listen. You think you aren't a ________________? Are you sure? Have you tried to write a poem? No? Well, try now. Have you had an ________________ with your ________________ and you're sad? Well, write it down and let it out. Then practise! At our poetry slams the ____________ is almost as important as the poem itself. But don't worry you'll get a bad ________________ – we show ________________ to all our slamsters. Winners can win a prize, but this isn't about prizes. It's about ________________.

Das englische Schulsystem

2 Welche Begriffe werden hier beschrieben? Setze aus den hinterlegten Buchstaben das Lösungswort zusammen.

1. English children go this school from the age of five. _ _ _ _ _ _ _ _ _ _ _ _ _
2. You usually go to this school for seven years. _ _ _ _ _ _ _ _ _ _ _ _ _
3. You need these exams before you go to university. _ _ _ _ _ _ _ _ _ _ _ _ _ _
4. Pupils go here when they are 16. _ _ _ _ _ _ _

→ Lösungswort: _ _ _ _ _ _ _ _ _ _ _ _ _ _

Was ist das?

3 Beschrifte die Bilder.

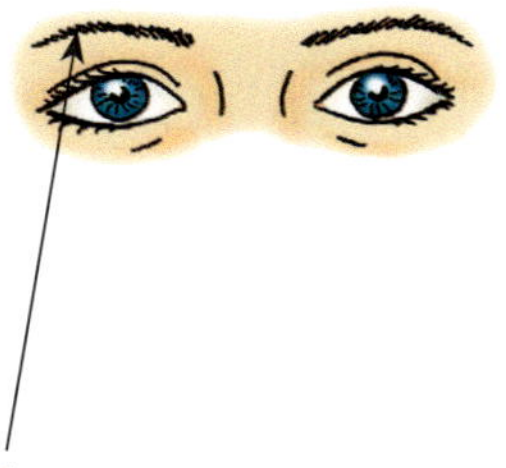
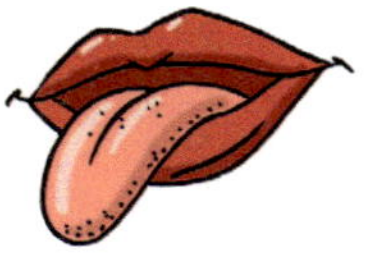

1. ____________________ 2. ____________________ 3. ____________________

4. ____________________ 5. ____________________ 6. ____________________

Adjektive: Gegenteile

4 Trage die Adjektive rechts jeweils so ein, dass sie gegenteilige Wortpaare bilden. Ein Adjektiv bleibt übrig – welches? Was bedeutet es?

____________	____________
____________	____________
____________	____________
____________	____________
____________	____________
____________	____________

alive **calm** **clever** **dead** **frustrated** **happy** **nervous** **sad** **strong** **stupid** **weak**

Verben

5 Manche Substantive benötigen ein bestimmtes Verb, mit dem sie stehen können. Ergänze die richtigen Verben im Text.

I sometimes think I should ______________ notes before I talk to my parents so that I don't say the wrong thing. I often ______________ an argument with them if I want to do something that they are not happy with. My mum ______________ into such a state when she sees my tattoo and my dad ______________ a fit when he sees my pierced nose. Maybe I shouldn't talk to them at all, I should just ______________ messages on the answering machine.

6 Suche die passenden Übersetzungen aus dem Wortgitter und ordne sie zu.

p	i	e	r	c	e	f	h	p	l
d	n	t	r	l	x	e	b	e	t
f	v	i	a	i	m	b	y	s	a
q	e	z	u	c	a	r	e	g	c
j	n	m	w	k	m	i	v	b	o
l	t	o	s	j	u	k	c	r	n
t	t	v	s	g	m	n	j	z	t
o	p	e	r	f	o	r	m	e	a
y	i	c	o	p	r	z	f	b	c
c	h	o	k	e	f	t	e	x	t

erfinden ______________

durchstechen ______________

klicken ______________

aufführen ______________

umziehen ______________

wetten ______________

sich kümmern ______________

sich in Verbindung setzen ______________

keine Luft bekommen ______________

eine SMS schicken ______________

Wichtige Wendungen: Wenn alles schiefgeht

7 Was kannst du sagen, wenn etwas falschläuft? Vervollständige die Sätze.

W _ a _ a _ i _ a _ _ e r!

I _’_ ju _ _ _ o _ _ a i _.

I _’s _ _ i _ i _ g _ e _ _ a _ y!

O _, t _ a _’_ _ e _ _ i b _ e.

_ e _ u s _ _ o _ o _ e _ _ i _ g!

Tipp Sprich die Sätze mehrfach laut aus: Irgendwann rollen sie dir wie von selbst von der Zunge.

8 Am Telefon. Verbinde die Satzteile zu vollständigen Sätzen.

1. I’m just calling to say	me back, please?
2. Could you call	it for me, please?
3. Can I take	I’ll be home late.
4. Can you spell	speak to Chris.
5. Sorry I can’t	take your call now.
6. I’d like to	a message?

9 Welche der Sätze aus Aufgabe 8 kann man benutzen, wenn man auf einen Anrufbeantworter spricht?

Es eignen sich die Sätze ____________________.

Wiederholung: Pronomen

Wenn du über Personen redest, kannst du Pronomen verwenden, statt immer den Namen zu nennen. Wenn du einen Besitz bezeichnen willst, verwendest du die Possessivbegleiter *my, your, he/she/it, our, your, their.*

Subjektpronomen	Objektpronomen	Reflexivpronomen
I am a girl.	Give it to **me.**	That's **mine.**
You are nice.	I like **you.**	Is that **yours?**
He is my friend.	I'll call **him** now.	That glass is **his.**
She is the umpire.	I haven't seen **her.**	The poem is **hers.**
It is a nice dog.	You can play with **it.**	The ball is **its.**
We are on the bus.	Can you meet **us?**	The cars are **ours.**
They are sisters.	Has he met **them?**	The song is **theirs.**

10 Bei einem *poetry slam*. Trage die richtigen Pronomen bzw. Begleiter ein.

1. – Gemma was nervous, wasn't she? She told __________ before the slam.

   \+ But __________ poem was very good, wasn't it?

   – Yes, __________ was. It was much better than __________. My poem wasn't very good. Has __________ written many poems?

   \+ Yes, __________ has. The poem in our school newspaper is __________.

2. – What do the winners win?

   \+ __________ win a place on a course. Famous poets give __________ lessons and somebody prints __________ poems.

3. – Well done! __________'ve won. __________ poem was great.

   \+ Thanks, but the poem wasn't __________.

   – What do you mean it wasn't __________?

   \+ John wrote it. It was __________. But __________ was too nervous to perform.

Wiederholung: das Futur

Dass etwas in der Zukunft passieren wird, kann man mit dem ***will-future***, dem ***going-to-future*** und dem ***present progressive*** ausdrücken.

Das ***will-future*** verwendest du, wenn du

– etwas vorhersagen willst, worauf du keinen Einfluss hast:	The weather **won't be** good today. People **will** always **play** football.
– deine Meinung abgibst. Dabei benützt du z. B. *I'm sure, I promise* oder *I think:*	I think we**'ll win** the competition. I hope it **won't snow** later.
– spontan etwas entscheidest:	Is that the phone? – Oh yes. I**'ll answer** it.

Das ***going-to-future*** verwendest du, wenn du

– einen Plan oder eine Absicht äußerst:	He**'s going to go** rowing next week. We**'re going to learn** some new tricks on the skateboard.
– etwas durch Anzeichen, die es jetzt schon gibt, vorhersehen kannst:	It's very cloudy and cold. It**'s going to snow** later. We**'re going to lose** the game.

Das ***present progressive*** verwendest du, wenn

– du mit jemandem etwas vereinbart hast:	I**'m meeting** John tomorrow.

11 Ein Umzug. Ergänze mithilfe der angegebenen Verben die Antwortsätze.

I have to move house. – (visit) ______________________.

Is that somebody at the door? – (look) ______________________.

I've got so many things. – (help) ______________________ pack.

Oh, these things are so heavy. – (carry) ______________________.

I'll miss you. – (phone) ______________________ every day.

Zuhören: Gegenwart oder Zukunft? 13

12 Höre dir die Kurzdialoge auf der CD an und vervollständige die Sätze. Bei welchen handelt es sich um eine spontane Reaktion?

	spontane Reaktion
1. Oh, I ____________ with you.	☑
2. Oh, I'm sure you ____________ win.	☐
3. No, I ____________ football with my friends then.	☐
4. ______________________ it to me?	☐
5. I ____________ you some new ones.	☐
6. I ____________ in the 100 metres.	☐
7. I ____________ 13 next Friday.	☐

13 Beim Tennis. Trage die richtige Form der Zukunft in die Lücken ein.

Wendy: Look! Yvonne is tired now. Liz ________________ (win) the match.

Chris: I don't know. Look at those clouds. We ________________ (have) a storm soon and then they ________________ (stop) the match.

Wendy: I hope they ______________________ (not/stop) stop the match.

Chris: Did you phone Tim? ____________________________ (you/meet) him later?

Wendy: Yes, I called him. He ________________ (come) here at three and we ______________________ (play) tennis. Do you want to play, too?

Chris: Oh, I think I ________________ (go) home. I don't want to get wet.

Wiederholung: Steigerung/Vergleich von Adjektiven und Adverben der Art und Weise

Du verwendest **Adverbien,** um auszudrücken, wie jemand etwas macht: He drives **badly.** Mit **Adjektiven** beschreibst du, wie etwas ist: He's a **bad** driver.

Du bildest die meisten Adverbien, indem du an das Adjektiv ***-ly*** hängst: cheap → cheaply.

Adverbien stehen meist nach dem Objekt: He eats **curry quickly.**

Wenn du Personen oder Dinge vergleichen möchtest, brauchst du die Steigerungsformen der Adjektive und Adverbien:

– Kurze Adjektive und Adverbien steigerst du mit ***-er*** und ***-est:*** Our new house is **bigger** than our old house. It is **the biggest** house in the street. Dad must work **harder** than before. He works **the hardest.**

– Längere Adjektive und Adverbien steigerst du mit ***more*** und ***most:*** Her voice is **more beautiful** than mine. She sings **the most beautifully** in the school.

– Vergleiche kannst du auch mit ***as … (not) as*** anstellen: I think she was **as** good **as** him, but she was**n't as** good **as** Ellen.

Es gibt unregelmäßige Adverbien, die du auswendig lernen musst: He sings **well** but he speaks **fast.** He tries **hard** and he talks **in a friendly way.**

Präge dir auch die unregelmäßigen Steigerungsformen ***well – better – best*** und ***badly – worse – worst*** ein.

14 Umgezogen. Streiche die jeweils falsche Formen durch.

I've just moved to a beautiful/beautifully place in Wales but I don't know if I like it here yet. I've met some nice/nicely kids at school but I miss my old/oldly friends terrible/terribly. I've found a good/well rap club so I can go there in the evening. Some of the kids play really good/well and I want to learn, too. Maybe if I try hard/hardly, I'll be happy/happily soon.

15 Sieh dir die Informationen über die drei *slamsters* an und vervollständige die Sätze.

- Liz – great poem
- performance – excellent
- audience response – very exited

- Susan – good poem
- performance – good
- audience response – good

- Paul – poem OK
- performance – OK
- audience response – OK

Liz's poem was __________ (good) and Paul's poem was __________ (bad). Susan performed __________ (beautiful) than Paul but Liz performed __________ (beautiful). The audience's response to Susan's poem was __________ (good) than to Paul's. The audience response to Liz's poem was __________ (excited).

16 Ergänze die richtige Form des Adjektivs bzw. Adverbs im Text.

John had an __________ (exciting) girlfriend but she left him because he was too __________ (boring) for her. John was __________ (sad) than ever before. He worked __________ (hard) than he had planned and wrote a poem. Was it __________ (good) than other poems? He didn't know but it said what he wanted to say. He was sitting __________ (quiet) at a poetry slam when he decided to let it out. He thought he must be the __________ (stupid) person in the room but he performed __________ (brilliant). Not a person in the room thought he was boring.

Wiederholung: Bedingungssätze mit *will*

Wenn etwas passieren **könnte** und du sagen willst, was dann passiert, verwendest du den Bedingungssatz mit *will* (Typ-1-Bedingungssatz).

Bedingung im *if*-Satz ***simple present***	**Folge im Hauptsatz** ***will future***
If it **rains** later,	I'**ll stay** at home.
If John and I **meet** today,	we'**ll watch** a film together.
If Jill **doesn't come** to my party,	I **won't be** happy.

Wenn man den Hauptsatz zuerst nennt, verwendet man kein Komma: What will you do if your dad doesn't give you any money? I won't be able to buy anything if I don't get any money.

Verwechsle ***when*** nicht mit ***if:*** **When** I meet Lucy, I'll ask her to my party. → Es ist sicher, dass ich Lucy treffen werde. Aber: **If** I meet Lucy, I'll ask her to my party. → Es ist nicht sicher, dass ich Lucy treffen werde ("falls …").

Weitere Bedingungssätze

Du kannst *if* auch durch die Konjunktionen *until – bis, as soon as – sobald, as long as – solange, before – bevor* und *while – während* ersetzen*:* I'll stay here **until** the game finishes. We'll stop **as soon as** it starts to rain.

17 Ein Rätsel. Kreuze die falschen Verbformen durch. Mit wem wird Jane ins Kino gehen?

If it rains on Saturday afternoon, Jane will go/goes to the cinema. She wants to go with Ben, Joe, Rosy and Carol, but if Ben will go/goes, Joe won't go – he doesn't like Ben. Jane loves funny films and scary films. If they will go/go to see a scary film, Rosy and Ben won't go/don't go and if they won't go/don't go to see a scary film, Carol won't go/doesn't go. Who will go/does go with her if they go to see a funny film?

→ Jane will go with ______________________________.

18 Meine Schwester. Verwende die angegebenen Wörter, um vollständige Bedingungssätze mit *will* zu bilden.

if – my sister's boyfriend – to ask – her – she – to marry – him

____

my dad – not – to be happy – if – she – to marry – him – soon

____

if – they – to marry – my sister – to leave – home

____

if – my sister – to leave – home – I – to have – my own room. Hurray.

____

I – to be – happy – if – I – to have – my own room – ?

____

19 Was machst du am Wochenende? Übersetze ins Englische.

Was machst du am Wochenende, wenn es regnet?

____

Ich werde meine Hausaufgabe machen, während es regnet.

____

Sobald es aufhört, werde ich rausgehen.

____

Wenn es dunkel wird, gehe ich wieder nach Hause.

____

Pronomen auf *-self/-selves*

Du kannst die Pronomen auf *-self/-selves* als Reflexivpronomen oder als verstärkende Pronomen verwenden.

reflexive Verwendung:

I can look after **myself.**	... auf *mich (selbst)* aufpassen.
Don't hurt **yourself.**	Tu *dir* nicht weh.
He/She/The cat washes **himself/herself/itself.**	Er/Sie/Die Katze wäscht *sich.*
Let's make **ourselves** some lunch.	Machen wir *uns* etwas zum Mittagessen.
Help **yourselves** to some food.	Nehmt *euch* vom Essen.
They only think of **themselves.**	Sie denken nur an *sich.*

Die Reflexivpronomen sind Objekt im Satz und beziehen sich immer auf das Subjekt.
Viele Verben, die im Deutschen reflexiv sind, sind im Englischen nicht reflexiv, z. B.: He's **changed.** – Er hat *sich* verändert. **Sit down!** – Setzen Sie *sich!*

verstärkende Verwendung:
Mit den Pronomen auf *-self/-selves* kannst du auch betonen, dass jemand etwas **selbst** getan hat:
I made that cake **myself!**
Did you really paint your room **yourselves?**

20 Trage die richtigen Relativpronomen ein.

I've just hurt ____________________.

Bye everybody! I hope you all enjoyed ____________________.

She often talks to ____________________.

They made that CD ____________________.

Jane! Don't drive ________________ crazy with that homework. Let me help.

Tipp Achtung bei *you:* Verwendest du es für eine *(yourself)* oder mehrere *(yourselves)* Personen?

21 Ein ganz normaler Tag? Streiche die Relativpronomen durch, wo man sie nicht benötigt.

It was Friday. I got up and then got dressed myself as always. I was late and had to hurry myself, as always. I went to school, worked hard and behaved myself – as always! I got home, sat down myself and relaxed myself – as always. My dad made dinner and hurt himself with a knife – as always. I ate dinner and got ready myself for youth club – as always – on a Friday! When I got to youth club, I met myself a girl. We laughed and enjoyed ourselves. I felt myself happy – as always. But nothing now was as always – everything had changed itself.

22 Schreibe die farbig markierten Sätze mit einem Pronomen auf *-self/-selves* neu, um das Subjekt zu verstärken.

Hey, you two. This card is really nice. Did you really make it?

____

That poem's great and guess what! John wrote it.

____

Will you ask him for me? I don't want to ask him.

____

Ann! I'm not helping you. You have to find it.

____

We're hungry. Can we cook dinner?

____

Zuhören: die Pronomen auf *-self/-selves* 14

23 Höre dir die Sätze auf der CD an. Welche Pronomen hörst du? Trage sie ein. Dann überlege: Werden sie verstärkend oder reflexiv verwendet? Kreuze an.

Pronomen	verstärkend	reflexiv
1. ______	☐	☐
2. ______	☐	☐
3. ______	☐	☐
4. ______	☐	☐
5. ______	☐	☐
6. ______	☐	☐

24 Ein Theaterstück. Übersetze die Sätze.

Wir haben das Stück selbst geschrieben.

____

Alle haben sich fertig gemacht.

____

Wir mussten uns beeilen.

____

Ich war der Star und konnte mich nicht entspannen.

____

Aber alle hatten Spaß.

____

Each other

Wenn du sagen willst, dass zwischen Personen etwas wechselseitig passiert, verwendest du *each other*.

They often help **each other.**	Sie helfen **einander** oft.
They met **each other** at 8.30.	Sie trafen **sich** um 8.30.
They looked at **each other.**	Sie schauten sich **gegenseitig** an.

Verwechsle nicht *each other* und *themselves!*

They helped themselves. – Sie haben sich beide selbst bedient.

They helped each other. – Sie haben einander geholfen.

Wenn man über mehr als zwei Personen redet, verwendet man *one another:* They talked to one another. – Sie redeten miteinander.

25 Sieh dir die Bilder an und vervollständige die Sätze mit *each other* oder *themselves.*

1. They met ______________________.

2. They looked at ______________________.

3. They looked at ______________________.

4. They taught ______________________ to build a boat.

5. They took photos of ______________________.

Ein Umzug

26 Lies zunächst den Text. Dann überlege, wann Richard den Brief an Mary geschrieben hat, und trage die Wochentage auf Englisch als Absatzüberschriften ein.

Dear Mary,
I'm writing a letter because our telephone isn't working yet, so I can't call anybody and I can't send an e-mail. And I haven't got any money left on my mobile card. It's Sunday today and yesterday was probably the worst day of my life. My uncle hurt himself in the morning so my aunt had to look after him all day and we had to carry almost everything ourselves. My mum and dad had a big argument. My mum said that she didn't want to move. My dad said that was OK because he didn't want to work. They didn't speak to each other for the rest of the day. We couldn't find the cat and almost had to leave her there. We found her just before we left. My sister has cried since yesterday morning. And I don't have anybody who I can talk to and laugh with so I'm writing this letter. I'd almost forgotten how you write letters.

____

Yesterday was the first day at my new school. Monday! My favourite day – I don't think. It was awful. Usually when you start a new school, you know other kids who are starting with you, but I didn't know anybody or anything. I couldn't find the classrooms and I couldn't even understand everybody because they all talk strangely. The other kids in the class try to be nice but I don't have any idea what they are talking about most of the time. I asked somebody if they have a hip hop or a rap club here but they didn't really know. There's a youth club here so if it's easy to find, I'll go on Friday. Somebody told me they're having a poetry slam there on Friday. What the heck is a poetry slam? I didn't ask because I felt a bit stupid. They think I know everything because I'm from London, and I don't want them to find out too early that I don't know anything!

____

I was too late to take the letter to the post office yesterday so I can write some more today. Our phone still doesn't work and this is our fifth day in our new house. I feel like I have moved back to the nineteenth century. There's no Underground here and not many buses. One time I was late for school because the bus had to wait for lots of sheep to cross the road! Can you imagine that? Really it was quite funny. By the way I found out today what a poetry slam is. People write poems and then read them to everybody. Then judges decide who the winner is. Why should anybody want to do that? It sounds like an English lesson! Anyway if I don't finish this letter now, you'll never get it.

You won't believe what I did yesterday! I took part in the poetry slam and I won a prize! I still can't believe it myself. It started like this. In English on Thursday we had to write poems about the summer or about something important to us. Of course, I wrote about when we moved house and what I felt about it. I've never enjoyed an English lesson so much. I wrote down everything that happened and that made me laugh and then it made me feel better. The English teacher read it and asked me to read it out in front of the class. I'm sure you can imagine how nervous I was. But when I started to read it out, I really enjoyed it. The whole class laughed at the funny parts and I felt like a star. At the end everybody was very quiet and then they clapped. After that the other kids talked to me more and I think they could understand me better. After the lesson the teacher told me more about the poetry slam and said I should enter. Well, I still didn't want to enter but I went to watch anyway. It was great. I listened to the other kids and I heard how the audience cheered and suddenly I wanted to take part, too. At the end a man asked if anybody else had a poem and I stood up. I didn't have my poem with me but I could remember it – all of it. At the end everybody cheered and I won a prize. And you know what my prize is? I can now take part in another poetry slam in London and there'll be some famous people there. I'm really excited. You'll have to come and watch, too. Oh, and by the way, our phone works now so I can get e-mails again but I've decided I quite like letters, so I'll send this one anyway.

Please write soon.
See you soon (I hope),
Richard

27 Fragen zum Text in Aufgabe 26. Welche Antwort passt? Trage jeweils den richtigen Buchstaben ein.

1. Why did Richard write the letter? ____________
   a) Because he loved letters.
   b) Because the phone didn't work.
   c) Because his English teacher told him to.
2. Why didn't Richard's parents talk to each other? ____________
   a) Because they couldn't find the cat.
   b) Because Richard's uncle hurt himself.
   c) Because they had a big argument.
3. What did Richard think about the other kids at school? ____________
   a) They wanted to be friendly.
   b) They didn't want to talk to him.
   c) They didn't like him because he came from London.

4. How does Richard get to school? ____________
   a) He goes by bus.
   b) He walks.
   c) He goes by underground.
5. When did Richard perform his poem the first time? ____________
   a) At the poetry slam.
   b) At home in front of his parents.
   c) In his English lesson.
6. Why did Richard take part in the poetry slam? ____________
   a) He wanted to win a prize.
   b) He liked it when the audience cheered.
   c) A man told him that he should take part.

28 Lies die Aussagen zum Text und kreuze richtig an.

	true	false	not in the text
1. Richard didn't know what a poetry slam was.	☐	☐	☐
2. There are no trains in Richard's new town.	☐	☐	☐
3. Richard likes hip hop and rap.	☐	☐	☐
4. Richard's class didn't like his poem.	☐	☐	☐

29 Suche aus Richards Brief die Sätze heraus, die den hier genannten entsprechen, und schreibe sie samt Angabe der Zeile ab.

Richard's mum and dad argued terribly.

____

Richard wants to go to the youth club on Friday but isn't sure he can find it.

____

Richard thinks that Mary can understand that he felt unsure of himself.

____

Zuhören: Vokale und Konsonanten 15

30 Lies dir zunächst die Wörter durch, dann höre dir die CD an. Welche Wörter werden gesprochen? Kreuze an.

1. had	☐	hat	☐	7. bet	☐	bed	☐
2. park	☐	bark	☐	8. sad	☐	said	☐
3. ship	☐	sheep	☐	9. harm	☐	ham	☐
4. chip	☐	cheap	☐	10. fit	☐	feet	☐
5. bring	☐	brink	☐	11. pet	☐	bet	☐
6. live	☐	life	☐	12. boat	☐	bought	☐

Zuhören und das Wesentliche verstehen 16

31 Ein Streit. Höre dir die CD an, dann verbinde die Sätze so, wie sie im Text vorkommen. Notiere zuletzt, ob Mum oder Nic den jeweiligen Satz sagt.

1. Can we talk	you'll have to stay at home in …
2. If you don't get home early …,	if do all your homework first.
3. I'm not interested in	what your friends' parents think.
4. Well, that's true, but	I won't be late again.
5. If we agree on a time together,	about last night?
6. I'll let you stay out later on Saturday	I worried about you last night.

1. ____________ 2. ____________ 3. ____________

4. ____________ 5. ____________ 6. ____________

Hörverstehen: Telefongespräche

Am Telefon ist es meist schwieriger, jemanden zu verstehen, weil man die Person nicht sieht. Mit etwas Übung wird es besser gehen, du kannst aber auch folgende Tipps beherzigen, um es dir leichter zu machen.

Wenn du direkt mit jemandem sprichst:
- Bitte deine/-n Gesprächspartner/-in zu wiederholen, was er/sie sagt, wenn du ihn/sie nicht verstanden hast.
- Wiederhole selbst, was du gehört hast, um sicherzustellen, dass du alles richtig verstanden hast.

Wenn du eine Nachricht auf dem AB abhörst:
- Höre dir die Nachricht so oft an, bis du sie verstehst.
- Mach dir Notizen.

Drei Telefongespräche 17

32 Höre dir die CD an und beantworte zu jedem Gespräch die Fragen. Höre dir die Dialoge so oft an, wie du willst!

Phone call 1:
a) Who does Kylie want to speak to? ____________

b) Where is she? ____________

c) What does Kylie want Ann to do? ____________

Phone call 2:
a) Who's calling? ____________

b) Why is she calling? ____________

c) When does she want her friend to call back? ____________

Phone call 3:
a) Who is calling? ____________

b) What's his phone number? ____________

c) What should Neil's dad do? ____________

Skills workshop 3

Hörverstehen üben

Vor dem Hören: Schau dir die Überschrift, Bilder oder andere Hinweise an, um schon vorher so viele Informationen wie möglich zu erhalten. Auch die Fragen, die zum Text gestellt werden, können dir nützliche Hinweise zum Inhalt geben. Wenn du gleich weißt, worum es geht, kommst du beim Hören leichter mit.

Während des Hören: Du brauchst nicht jedes einzelne Wort zu verstehen – konzentriere dich auf den Gesamtzusammenhang! Mach dir eventuell Notizen: Vielleicht kannst du im Stillen schon die eine oder andere der folgenden Fragen beantworten. Dann höre dir den Text ein zweites Mal an und löse die Aufgaben dazu.

Schau dir **zum Schluss** deine Antworten nochmals an. Wenn du Lücken hast, rate – aber prüfe, ob die Antworten untereinander stimmig sind und sich nicht widersprechen.

Am wichtigsten: Lass dich nicht herausbringen, wenn du ein Wort oder einen Abschnitt nicht verstehst!

Zuhören: ein Theaterstück 18

1 Höre dir die drei Szenen auf dem CD-Track an. Wo befanden sich die Personen jeweils? Wähle die richtige Antwort.

a) At home. Sue is sitting in an armchair and she's watching TV. Her mum is standing near the door.
b) At home. Sue is sitting in an armchair and she's watching TV. She's wearing different clothes and she's just got up. Somebody has just knocked at the door.
c) In a shop. They're looking at clothes. It's Saturday and there are lots of other people there.

Scene 1: ________ Scene 2: _______ Scence 3: ________

2 Höre dir den Text ein zweites Mal an, wenn nötig, und beantworte die folgenden Fragen zum Text.

1. What did Sue want to buy?
   a) A dress. ☐
   b) A skirt. ☐
   c) Trousers. ☐
2. Who was Sue's boyfriend with? a) Jane. ☐ b) Sue. ☐ c) Chris. ☐
3. Sue doesn't want to talk to Jane because Jane …
   a) called her too often. ☐
   b) was in her favourite shop. ☐
   c) went out with Steve. ☐
4. Jane was in the shop because she was …
   a) looking for a dress. ☐
   b) helping Steve buy a present. ☐
   c) looking for clothes for Steve. ☐
5. Does Steve know that Sue was angry? a) Not in the text. ☐
   b) Yes. ☐ c) No. ☐

3 Welche Person sagt diese Sätze aus dem Text – Chris, Sue, Sues Mutter oder Jane? Ordne zu.

1. Hey, what do you think about these? ____________
2. What are they doing together? ____________
3. You must eat something. You haven't eaten all day. ____________
4. They weren't thinking about me. ____________
5. Happy Birthday! ____________

Test practice B

The new training shoes

"Do you really need new training shoes, Oliver? I bought you a new pair last week," says Dad.

"Dad, I don't understand you. You want me to do sport but you don't want me to have any trainers. You know we need shoes for inside and outside, don't you?"

"Sorry, Oliver, but money's a problem at the moment. You know we've just had to spend a lot of money on the house."

"Yeah, I know. Could I just have fifty pounds then, please?"

"Fifty pounds? For training shoes? No way. I'll tell you what. I'll come with you."

"What? Oh Dad! I'm fourteen."

"Well, buy them yourself then," says Dad.

Two hours later Oliver and his dad are in a sports shop.

"Can I help you?" asks the shop assistant.

"Yeah, we're looking for some training shoes," says Dad.

"For indoors or outdoors?"

"For indoors," says Oliver.

"For badminton, indoor football, tennis, ...?" asks the shop assistant.

"Well, I need some for badminton, some for football and some for ...," says Oliver but his dad stops him.

"Why should anybody get so many pairs of shoes?" asks his dad loudly.

"Well, when you play badminton you have to stop fast so ..." the shop assistant tries to answer.

"We'd just like some all-round trainers, OK?" said Dad.

Oliver tries on about four pairs. He finds the perfect pair and wants to buy them, when his dad notices the price.

"If you want them, you'll have to buy them yourself," says Dad. "Look at all those over there. They're half the price."

"Yes, but I won't buy any with that name; they use child labour."

"Child labour?" Oliver's dad can't believe his ears. "What do you mean?"

"Children make them. In India. Pakistan. Lots of countries. Children who are nine, ten and eleven years old work in factories all day and make them so that we can have cheap trainers."

"You're joking," says his dad. "How do you know all that?"

"I saw a programme on it yesterday. We are doing a project on it at school. We've still got it on DVD. You can watch it if you like, Dad."

"Well, I feel sorry for all the children and I don't think they should have to work but I'm not paying so much for trainers when I can buy some for half the price. It won't make any difference to them if we don't buy these shoes. They've already made them anyway."

"I can't believe you're saying that, Dad! And anyway I won't wear shoes that kids who are younger than me and who should be in school have made."

"Well, buy them yourself," says Dad.

"I know. I'll buy them. But you watch the programme when we get home. If you agree with me when you've watched the programme, you'll give me the money back. OK?"

Three hours later Oliver has got his money back again.

Reading

1 Sind die Aussagen zum Text *true, false* oder *not in the text?*

	true	false	not in the text
1. Oliver always needs two pairs of trainers.	☐	☐	☐
2. Oliver's parents don't have much money now.	☐	☐	☐
3. Oliver wants to go shopping with his dad.	☐	☐	☐
4. There are special trainers for many different sports.	☐	☐	☐
5. Oliver chooses the most expensive trainers.	☐	☐	☐
6. Only children in India make the trainers.	☐	☐	☐
7. Oliver watched a programme about child labour at school.	☐	☐	☐

2 Korrigiere die Aussagen aus Aufgabe 1, die du als *false* markiert hast.

Language

3 Suche aus dem Text die Sätze und Wendungen heraus, die den folgenden entsprechen, und nenne die Zeile dazu.

1. You pay for them with your money. ______________________
2. Do you need them for inside or outside? ______________________
3. They're a lot cheaper. ______________________
4. That's not true, is it? ______________________
5. Oliver's dad does not believe what he hears.

____

6. I feel bad about the children.

____

7. It won't change anything for the children.

____

Passing on information

4 Du gehst mit deiner Mutter, die schlecht Englisch spricht, in London shoppen. Erzähle ihr, was in der Werbeanzeige für die Turnschuhe steht.

– Look after your feet with our trainers
– Great for most inside sports: badminton, table tennis, tennis
– Made without child labour!

____

____

____

____

____

____

Listening 19

5 Höre dir die Unterhaltung auf der CD an und beantworte die Fragen dazu.

1. Was denkt Mary, Olivers Schwester? Kreuze die richtigen Aussagen an.

a) If we buy the shoes, the children will have more money. ☐

b) It's better for the children to work than go to school. ☐

c) Parents shouldn't have to work. ☐

2. Was denkt Oliver? Kreuze die richtigen Aussagen an.

a) They'll pay adults more money. ☐

b) They should pay more for theirs shoes if they need to. ☐

c) They should try to solve problems. ☐

Writing

6 Verfasse einen Text für ein Plakat gegen Kinderarbeit. Verwende dazu die angegebenen Wörter und Wendungen.

change children's lives | **firms use child labour** | **children not have to work** | **choose** | **think** | **give jobs to parents**

____

____

____

____

____

Unit 4

Regionen Großbritanniens

1 Ergänze die Lücken mit den passenden Wörtern.

coal mines – coastline – factories – industry – landscape – mountains – region – waterfront

The northwest of England is famous for its ________________ – the Industrial Revolution started here and one reason for this was all the coal in the area. Most of the ________________ are now closed but there are still many ________________ here. But it is also a beautiful ________________. Away from the cities the ______________ is wild with many ______________ and lakes. The ________________ is lovely, too, and there are some great beaches along it. And you should not miss Liverpool's ________________.

2 Bilde aus den Wortteilen ganze Wörter und trage sie richtig ein.

coa	sin	sk	trad	smug
y	glers	st	gers	ition

The Welsh ________________ is beautiful with many cliffs and beaches.

There were once many ________________ along the coast.

It does rain a lot so you often see clouds in the ________________.

There is a strong ________________ of music in Wales.

In fact many famous ________________ and actors come from Wales.

Bilder

3 Beschrifte die Bilder.

1. ______________ 2. ______________ 3. ______________ 4. ______________

5. ______________ 6. ______________ 7. ______________ 8. ______________

Brüche

4 Schreibe diese Brüche in Worten aus.

$\frac{1}{4}$ ______________________ $\frac{3}{4}$ ______________________

$\frac{1}{2}$ ______________________ $1\frac{1}{2}$ ______________________

Adjektive

5 Löse die Anagramme auf und ergänze damit sinnvoll die Substantive.

ninpedetend – anciten – plehessl – avulebla

a ____________________ painting an ____________________ woman

a ____________________ baby an ____________________ building

Verben

6 Die Sinne. Übersetze die gefragten Verben.

1. riechen ______________
2. klingen ______________
3. aussehen ______________
4. fühlen ______________
5. schmecken ______________
6. hören ______________
7. schauen ______________
8. scheinen ______________
9. berühren ______________

7 Finde in dem Buchstabengitter neun Verben und ordne sie jeweils ihrer Übersetzung zu.

festnehmen: ______________

klettern: ______________

sich ausruhen: ______________

schützen: ______________

definieren: ______________

stören: ______________

vertrauen: ______________

zupfen: ______________

beschädigen: ______________

s	a	c	l	i	m	b	d
d	e	f	i	n	e	o	g
a	w	z	j	h	i	t	r
m	l	t	u	g	y	h	e
a	b	r	s	e	q	e	k
g	a	u	r	h	b	r	u
e	l	s	c	a	t	c	h
q	a	t	m	s	z	d	n
n	j	u	z	r	x	s	e
p	r	o	t	e	c	t	a
m	d	n	r	s	g	m	i
r	h	e	i	t	k	a	l

Präpositionen

8 Trage die gefragten Präpositionen ein.

My mum had to go _______ for a few days so we had to look _______ ourselves and the house. My mum usually organises everything so everything went wrong while she was away. We got _______ late every day and were always late for school. We never put our shoes _______ when we took them _______ so we couldn't find them again later. One day we looked _______ my sister's shoes for 20 minutes. When she got _______ school, she saw that she had put _______ two different ones. My dad's a terrible cook and had to look _______ the recipes for anything he cooked. One day while he was cooking spaghetti bolognaise, all the lights went _______. We got takeaways after that. My mum came back on the Friday. She came in the door, looked _______ the kitchen and walked out again. "Call me again when it's clean," she said, "I'll be ____ your grandma's house."

9 Wo und wohin? Ergänze die richtigen Präpositionen.

1. One cat is ____________ the house and another one is ____________ it.

2. She went ____________ house and then walked ____________ it again.

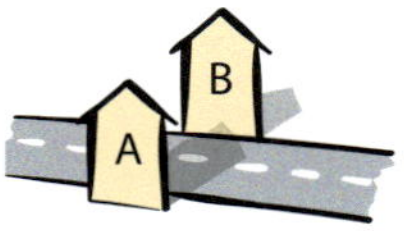

3. House A is ______________ house B.

Wichtige Wendungen: unterwegs

10 In der Touristeninformation. Bilde aus den Satzteilen Sätze und trage sie an den richtigen Stellen ein.

I'd like to know	about smugglers in the area?
I need to find a hotel	if there are any good museums here.
Do you have any information	which isn't too expensive.

+ ______________________________

– Yes, there's a really interesting one in the city centre.

+ ______________________________

– Why don't you try the Midland? That doesn't cost too much.

+ ______________________________

– Yes, we do. Would you like some leaflets?

11 Bilde aus den angegebenen Wörtern vollständige Fragen.

tell – Swansea – could – to – you – the time – me – of – the next train – please – ?

____

does – platform – from – what – it – leave – ?

____

change – I – trains – have – do – to – ?

____

a – airport – bus – is – there – to – the – ?

____

Relativsätze mit *whose*

Relativsätze sind Nebensätze, die etwas oder jemanden näher bestimmen oder zusätzliche Informationen geben. Sie werden durch **Relativpronomen** eingeleitet, z. B. ***who, that*** oder ***whose.***

Mit *whose* drückst du einen **Besitz** aus. Man kann es für Menschen oder Dinge verwenden:

I know a boy **whose** brother plays rugby for Wales. – Ich kenne einen Jungen, dessen Bruder für Wales Rugby spielt.

Der Relativsatz kann manchmal auch in der Mitte des Hauptsatzes stehen:

Some children **whose** parents speak Welsh learn Welsh before English. – Manche Kinder, **deren** Eltern Walisisch sprechen, lernen Walisisch vor Englisch.

Achtung: Verwechsle *whose* nicht mit *who's (who is)!*

12 Bilde aus den zwei Sätzen jeweils einen einzigen Satz mit *whose.*

1. Shirley Bassey is a famous Welsh singer. Her father came from Nigeria.

____

2. Wales is a country. Its road signs are usually in two languages.

____

3. Most people speak English, too. Their first language is Welsh.

____

Zuhören: *who's* oder *whose?* 20

13 Höre dir den CD-Track an. Wird *who's* oder *whose* gesprochen?

1. ____________ 3. ____________

2. ____________ 4. ____________

Das Stützwort *one/ones* nach Adjektiven

Wenn du ein Nomen nicht wiederholen möchtest, musst du stattdessen – im Gegensatz zum Deutschen – ***one/ones*** verwenden:

Which is your house? – The biggest **one.**
Those shoes are nice. – Yes, and the red **ones** are the nicest.

Du musst ***one*** oder ***ones*** immer mit einem Adjektiv, mit *this/that, Which?* oder einem Ausdruck wie *on the left, under the book* näher erklären:

Which **one** is yours? – Mine is that **one** over there. The **one** on the table.

14 Beim Einkaufen. Schreibe *one* oder *ones* in die Lücken.

1. How much are the apples? – The green ________ or the red ________?
2. I'd like to look at that bag. – Which ________? The big, brown ________?
3. How much are those sandwiches? – These cheese ________ are £1.50.

15 In einem Souvenirladen. Übersetzte die farbig markierten Teile der Dialoge.

1. Was kosten die Postkarten? – Die großen kosten 30 Pence.

____

2. Das Poster ist toll. – Das an der Wand?

____

3. Kann ich mir bitte den Füller ansehen? – Welchen? Diesen?

____

4. Kann ich bitte das T-Shirt anprobieren? – Dieses gelbe?

____

5. Die Tassen sind schön. – Meinst du die da drüben?

____

Relativsätze mit *who, which* oder *that*

Mit einem notwendigen Relativsatz wird ein Wort **näher beschrieben.** Ohne ihn wäre der Sinn des Hauptsatzes unklar.

Personen	*subject*	
I like **the teacher** I don't know **anybody**	**who/that** **who/that**	teaches us Welsh. can ski well.
Dinge	*subject*	
Rugby is **a game** He won **a competition**	**which/that** **which/that**	is very popular in Britain. is held every two years.

Who bezieht sich nur auf Menschen, ***which*** nur auf Dinge, ***that*** kann sich auf Menschen oder Dinge beziehen.

Vor einem notwendigen Relativsatz steht *kein* Komma, und beim Sprechen gibt es *keine* Pause zwischen Hauptsatz und Relativsatz.

Der Relativsatz kann auch das **Objekt** des Satzes näher beschreiben:

The sport **which/that** I like best is rugby. – Den Sport, den ich am liebsten mag, ist Rugby.
That's the girl **who/that** we met yesterday. – Das ist das Mädchen, das wir gestern getroffen haben.

When ***which, that*** oder ***who*** das Objekt beschreiben, können sie auch entfallen:

That's the girl we met yesterday. The sport I like best is rugby.

16 Sport! Ergänze *who, whose* oder *which*.

People __________ become very good at sport have to train very hard for many years. It helps if they have a sports club __________ is good in their area. And it's always easier for children __________ friends like sport, too. There are also people __________ have bodies __________ are better for one sport or another. For example, people __________ legs are longer are often better at running. And, of course, for some sports it's easier for children __________ parents can buy them good equipment or lessons.

17 In Wales. Formuliere vollständige Sätze mit *who, whose* oder *which*.

1. I met some people – they were very nice

I met ______________________________

2. I heard some music – it was great

____

3. I stayed with people – their mother sang in a famous choir

____

4. I visited some beaches – they were beautiful

____

5. The people owned the hotel – they spoke English and Welsh

____

18 Golfspielen. Markiere beim ersten Lesen die Relativpronomen. Dann lies den Text nochmals und streiche die Relativpronomen durch, die man nicht unbedingt braucht (also wenn sie Objekt des Relativsatzes sind).

Golf is a sport which is very popular in England but it is not a sport that most people think is very exciting. In fact there are people who think that golf isn't a sport at all because they think of old people who walk slowly around a big field or two and every ten minutes or so hit a ball. I was once one of those people. I'm a person who loves most sport but I thought that golf was very boring. How wrong I was! A friend who I've known for years and loves golf bought me a lesson for my birthday. It was a present which I didn't really want but you can't say no, can you? And I'm glad I didn't say, "No, thank you," because it was one of the best presents that I've ever had. I loved the lesson and I've loved golf ever since. It's great fun when you play with people who you like and it makes you healthy. You often walk ten kilometres or more in places which are very tiring while you are carrying a bag which is very heavy.

Lesen: ein Segelurlaub

19 Lies die Geschichte einmal durch, um das Wesentliche zu verstehen. Dann entscheide dich für die beste Zusammenfassung.

"I asked my mum if I could go on the sailing holiday," said Mary after she'd arrived at Julia's house.
"And what did she say?" asked Julia.
"Well, she said I could learn to sail here."
"But it's much more exciting to sleep in a boat on the sea."
"Yes, I know. I told her. And I think she understood that but she still thinks I'm too young."
"So you can't come?"
"Yes, I can. My dad talked to her. Good old dad!" cried Mary happily.
"Oh, great," said Julia, "I'm so excited. Four weeks and we can go. I wonder if we'll meet some nice people there."
"I hope so. Do you think the sea will be warm?" asked Mary, and they talked about it all night.

It was the fifth of August and Julia and Mary had been on the *Good Hope* for two days.
"How are you?" asked Julia.
"Oh, I still feel terrible," said Mary. "I can't believe it. Why do I still feel sick? I've been on boats lots of times – OK, maybe not such a small one – but I've never felt sick before."
"Well, just relax. You'll feel better soon. The captain said you'll feel better soon."
Mary just stood on the boat and looked at the sea. She felt better like that. She hadn't sailed herself at all up to then, but she watched the others and so she'd learnt things. She was still glad that she'd come because the weather was good and they met some people who were great fun.
On the sixth of August she woke up early and felt different. What was it? Then she knew. She didn't feel sick any more. She jumped up out of her bed, which was the top one, and banged her head. "Ow," she cried, but it didn't stop her. She ran outside and joined the others who were all eating breakfast. They all cheered when they saw that she no longer felt sick. And the rest of the day was wonderful. They all worked together well as a team and Mary could help now, too. The wind became stronger and the boat flew over the waves. It was a fantastic feeling. But it didn't last long.
The wind became stronger and stronger and they had to put the sails down so that they could control the boat. The sky went dark with black clouds and the waves became bigger and bigger. Mary started to feel sick again, but even worse, it scared her, too.

"Put your life jackets *(Schwimmwesten)* on now," said the captain. "A storm is coming."
Everybody put their life jackets on. The captain had heard about the storm on the radio but it had come more quickly than he had thought – and it was worse.
There was nothing they could do. They just had to wait. It got darker and darker – night was coming, and there was no sign of the end of the storm. Nobody was laughing now or even talking. Then suddenly they heard a loud crash and the boat jumped. They had hit something. The captain used the radio and called for help quickly. He looked over the side of the boat. There was a hole *(Loch)* in it but it was a small one.
They waited and waited. Could anybody come out in this storm? Then they heard a helicopter and saw its lights. It came nearer and nearer but then turned around and went back again. There was nothing it could do. A short time later they heard a lifeboat *(Rettungsboot)*. They saw the lights. They got nearer and nearer but then they stopped.
"I don't think they can come nearer in this weather," said the captain, "the cliffs are too near."
Nobody spoke. The water in the boat was rising and the boat was going down.
"Why didn't I stay at home?" thought Mary.

mögliche Zusammenfassungen:
A) Mary and Julia go on holiday by boat. Before they arrive, there's a bad storm and Mary feels sick.
B) Mary and Julia stay on a boat on the sea on holiday. There's a terrible storm and Mary feels sick.
C) Mary and Julia learn to sail on holiday. Mary feels sick at first and later there's a bad storm.

Die beste Zusammenfassung ist __________.

20 Lies die Fragen durch und wähle jeweils die richtige Antwort.

1. Why didn't Mary's mum want her to go on holiday? → __________
a) She thought it was dangerous.
b) She thought Mary was too young.
c) She thought it was too expensive.

2. When did Mary feel better? → __________
a) On the second day.
b) On the third day.
c) On the fourth day.

3. When did the storm come? → ________
a) On the fifth of August.
b) On the sixth of August.
c) On the seventh of August.

4. What did the captain do when the boat hit something? → ________
a) Put lifejackets on.
b) Went inside.
c) Called for help.

5. What came out in the storm? → ________
a) A helicopter.
b) A lifeboat.
c) A helicopter and a lifeboat.

21 Was bedeutet *one* in den angegebenen Zeilen? Nenne das englische Wort.

1. … OK, maybe not such a small **one** … (line 18) ____________

2. … which was the top **one** and banged her head (line 28). ____________

3. … but it was a small **one** (line 48). ____________

22 Die Geschichte geht gut aus: Alle werden gerettet. Schreibe die Geschichte zu Ende und verwende dafür die rechts angegebenen Notizen.

____
____
____
____
____
____
____

wait **became cold** **more water in boat** **wind: less strong** **boat: hit cliffs** **lifeboat: saved**

Zuhören: der Laut [s] 21

23 Lies dir die Wörter durch und kreuze an: Welche Wörter werden mit stimmhaftem s, also [s], gesprochen? Erst dann prüfe deine Antworten mithilfe der CD.

stone	☐	smuggler	☐	observatory	☐	circle	☐
ancient	☐	side	☐	landscape	☐	sheet	☐
singer	☐	customs	☐	zoo	☐	suitcase	☐

Zuhören: Bitten äußern 22

24 Höre dir die drei Kurzdialoge auf der CD an. In welchem Dialog hörst du die hier genannten Sätze?

1. Do you have any information about the museums here? ____________
2. Excuse me. ____________
3. Here's a map for you. ____________
4. Sorry to bother you, but could I sit there? ____________
5. Could you close the window, please? ____________
6. Oh, that's no problem. ____________

25 Jetzt beantworte die Fragen zu den Dialogen auf CD-Track 22.

1. Dialogue 1: Does the boy close the window? ____________________
2. Dialogue 2: What does the woman do? ____________________
3. Dialogue 3: What does the girl want? ____________________
4. Dialogue 3: What does the woman give her? ____________________

Zuhören: ein Umzug 23

26 Höre dir das Telefongespräch an, dann entscheide dich: Welche Beschreibung passt am besten dazu?

a) Luke has moved house and is talking to his friend Lisa on the phone. ☐

b) Luke is going to move house and has just been to visit their new house. ☐

c) Luke is going on holiday for the whole summer. ☐

Tipp Du brauchst nicht jedes Wort zu verstehen, um den Sinn einer Unterhaltung zu erfassen. Wenn du bestimmte Informationen suchst, konzentriere dich auf die relevanten Wörter.

27 Lies zunächst die Fragen durch, dann höre dir den CD-Track 23 nochmals an. Welche Antwort ist richtig?

1. Where's Luke going to move to?
a) Brighton ☐
b) Bristol ☐
c) Birmingham ☐

2. Where are they going to live?
a) in the country ☐
b) on a hill ☐
c) near the sea ☐

3. When are they going to move?
a) the end of June ☐
b) the end of July ☐
c) the end of August ☐

4. Who's Luke meeting on his birthday?
a) Jill ☐
b) friends from his old school ☐
c) friends from his new school ☐

5. When will Luke forget Jill?
a) at Christmas ☐
b) before Christmas ☐
c) after Christmas ☐

Skills workshop 4

Reading skills: Sachtexte

Wenn du nach bestimmten Informationen suchst, also z. B. an einem Projekt arbeitest oder ein passendes Urlaubsziel ausfindig machen möchtest, liest du Sachtexte *(factual texts)*. Um festzustellen, ob und wie sie dir hilfreich sein können, gibt es zwei Methoden.

Skimming **(Überfliegen):** Zunächst überfliegst du den Text nur, denn du willst nur ungefähr wissen, wovon er handelt. Außerdem muss es schnell gehen, denn vielleicht ist der Text für dich gar nicht interessant. Achte nur auf Schlüsselwörter, z. B. Verben und Substantive.

Scanning **(Durchsuchen nach Details):** Wenn du den richtigen Text gefunden hast, suchst du gezielt nach bestimmten Informationen. Du überfliegst also den Text ein zweites Mal, aber diesmal fahndest du ganz konkret nach bestimmten Wörtern.

1 William, Ellen, Maria und Liam möchten Urlaub machen. „Skimme" die Texte: Welche beiden Orte könnten jeweils für welche Person interessant sein?

William wants to walk in the country. He likes the water. ____________

Ellen wants to go on a short break to a city. ____________

Maria likes the country and wants to relax. ____________

Liam wants to visit a city and the country. ____________

A: Isle of Wight

The Isle of Wight is a small island off the south coast of England. The two biggest towns on the island are Newport, its capital, and Ryde, where most people arrive by boat. There are also many smaller villages around the island, most

of them on the coast. The Isle of Wight has not changed a lot in the last fifty years and it is an ideal place for people who like to enjoy life slowly and for people who love the sea and walks in beautiful country.
There are beautiful beaches all around the island but they are different on the different coasts. If you enjoy surfing or windsurfing and big waves, try the west of the island. If you like empty beaches to enjoy by yourself, try the south of the island. The best place for sailing is Cowes on the north coast.
The Isle of Wight has no mountains but it is a hilly place and a great place to cycle and walk. The weather also helps as the Isle of Wight is one of the sunniest places in Great Britain.
There are also many interesting places to visit on the Isle of Wight. You can visit many historical places such as castles and Roman ruins. Or try a theme park, the zoo or one of the many museums here.

B: Newcastle
Many tourists to England don't get as far north as Newcastle – and they miss a lot. Newcastle has a lot to offer but it is probably most famous for its nightlife. It has maybe the best nightlife in England. It is a small city and so it's easy to visit a lot of places in a short time. There are many theatres, nightclubs, discos, bars and restaurants. There is something for anybody who likes to go out in the evening or who likes music. Try one of the nightclubs by the river and if you go at the right time of year, you can also go to one of the many festivals in Newcastle. But don't take a coat with you or you'll look like a tourist – even in winter "Geordies" (the local people from Newcastle) usually go out just in shirts or dresses.

It is not only the nightlife which is interesting: Newcastle is great for shopping, too. It also has many museums, art galleries, historically interesting places and its football club. The football club is important in Newcastle. Many Geordies love football and on Saturdays you don't need to see the score to know if Newcastle has won or not.
If you want to get out of the city for a day, there are many interesting and beautiful places to choose from. Newcastle is near the coast and so for anybody
who is interested in water sports, it is a great place to visit. There are also some great country parks nearby for people who like a walk in the country.

C: The Lake District
The Lake District is in the northwest of England. As you can see by the name, there are many lakes here and there are also many mountains. The

Lake District is very popular with British walkers and climbers; the sporty and the not-so-sporty. You could spend years walking in the Lake District and not have to walk on the same path twice. The not-so-sporty can walk around lakes, have tea and return by boat.

The Lake District is also by the coast and so it is an interesting place for people who like water sports of any kind. You can canoe or sail in the sea, the rivers or in the lakes here. You can swim or dive. And if you don't like sport at all, you can just sit and enjoy the beautiful views. The Lake District is mostly famous because the country is so wild and beautiful. Many English poets came here in the nineteenth century to write, and many people also come to visit the places that they wrote about or the places in which they wrote.

There are no very big towns in the Lake District, and although there are interesting places here to visit, it is really a place for people who love to be outside. And for people who don't mind the rain: the Lake District is one of the wettest places in Great Britain.

D: Bristol

Bristol is a very interesting city historically and was one of England's biggest cities until the Industrial Revolution. The Romans settled here and you can still see Roman ruins here or at the nearby town, Bath. Later Bristol, which is in the west of England, became an important harbour as people started to sail to America.

Bristol is a very attractive city and a place which is easy to enjoy. The River Avon runs through the middle and you can go on boat trips through the city and out into the country. There are lots of things to do in Bristol and places to visit; museums, shops, theatres, cinemas – but it is also a place where you can just sit and relax. It has a good nightlife, too, and Bristol is famous for its music and film industries.

Bristol is also a perfect place from which to visit South Wales and Cornwall, Devon and Dorset. You can go by rail, by car or bus and visit many interesting places for the day. For anybody who is coming from a different country, Bristol is easy to get to, by train or by plane.

2 Lies weitere Informationen über William, Ellen, Maria und Liam. Dann „scanne“ die Texte, die du in Aufgabe 1 jeweils ausgesucht hattest, und überlege, welcher der Orte eher die Interessen abdeckt: Welcher Urlaubsort ist am geeignetsten?

William loves …
- mountains
- sailing
- canoeing
- the sea

→ ______________

Maria loves …
- mountains
- surfing
- historical places
- the sea

→ ______________

Ellen loves …
- music
- films
- historical places
- shopping

→ ______________

Liam loves …
- music
- nightclubs
- football
- the sea

____

3 Lies den Text in Aufgabe 1 nochmals und beantworte dann die Fragen dazu.

1. Where is the Isle of Wight? ______________
____
2. How much has it changed in the last 50 years? ______________
3. What can you do in the west of the island? ______________
4. Where's Newcastle? ______________
____
5. What's Newcastle most famous for? ______________
6. What do many Geordies love? ______________
7. Where's the Lake District? ______________

8. What can you do there? ______________________
____

9. What's the weather like? ______________________

10. Which places are easy to visit from Bristol? ______________________

11. What is Bristol famous for? ______________________
____

12. Where did people sail to from Bristol? ______________________

4 Sind die Aussagen *true, false* oder *not in the text?* Korrigiere dann die Sätze, die falsch sind.

	true	false	not in the text
1. There are many cliffs on the Isle of Wight.	☐	☐	☐
2. It doesn't rain much on the Isle of Wight.	☐	☐	☐
3. Many tourists visit Newcastle.	☐	☐	☐
4. A river runs through Newcastle.	☐	☐	☐
5. You have to be very fit to walk in the Lake District.	☐	☐	☐
6. You can swim in all the lakes in the Lake District.	☐	☐	☐
7. Bristol doesn't have an airport.	☐	☐	☐

Korrektur: ____
____
____

Revision B (Unit 3–4)

Odd one out

1 Finde jeweils die Person bzw. Sache, die nicht in die Reihe passt.

1. luggage
   trolley
   suitcase
   rucksack

→ ____________

2. bloke
   prince
   boyfriend
   poet

→ ____________

3. monastery
   basement
   attic
   hall

→ ____________

4. beard
   tongue
   aftershave
   eyebrow

→ ____________

5. sky
   mountain
   cliff
   channel

→ ____________

6. singer
   owner
   choir
   judge

→ ____________

Zwei-Wort-Verben

2 Stelle Zwei-Wort-Verben zusammen und ergänze sie in den Sätzen.

hang	hold	take	put	go
away	out	out	up	off

1. At a poetry slam the judges ____________ a piece of paper with the number of points on it.
2. Where do you ____________ on a Friday? – Oh, at the youth club.
3. Can you ____________ your shoes and then ____________ in the cupboard, please?
4. When the lights ____________ at the cinema, the film starts.

Adjektive

3 Ordne die acht Adjektive richtig den Sätzen zu.

independent – weak – unfair – ancient – helpless – safe – calm – frustrated

1. The mountains are very old. They're ________________.
2. She can look after herself. She's very ________________.
3. You can think better if you stay ________________.
4. He's ________________. He can't do anything himself.
5. She was the best but she didn't win. That's ________________.
6. He's very ________________. He's tried again and again but he still can't do it.
7. She isn't strong. She's very ________________.
8. If it's not dangerous, it's ________________.

Wer oder was?

4 Trage *who, whose* oder *which* ein und ergänze, wer/was beschrieben wird.

1. The person t__________ lives in a house isn't always the o________________.
2. The t________________ is something __________ you talk with.
3. s________________ are people __________ take things they shouldn't into countries.
4. A c________________ is a small building __________ you can live in.
5. A p________________ is a person __________ father is usually the king.
6. A m________________ is something __________ you can see yourself in.

Reflexivpronomen

5 Ein Umzug. Übersetze.

1. Wir haben fast alles selbst tragen müssen.

____

2. Ich habe mich verletzt, als ich mich auf einen kaputten Stuhl gesetzt habe.

____

3. Ich kann meine alten Freunde jetzt nicht treffen, aber wir schreiben uns.

____

4. Ich komme zwar allein klar (= „kann auf mich aufpassen"), aber ich fühle mich traurig.

____

Urlaub in Großbritannien

6 Verbinde die Satzhälften zu sinnvollen Sätzen.

We're going to stay in the most	which we can sail ourselves.
We're going to stay in a village	we'll go swimming a lot.
There are many mountains there	beautiful cottage you have ever seen.
We're going to meet a friend	if they have time to help me.
I'll try to learn Welsh	which is near the sea.
I think Welsh people speak English	whose parents are Welsh.
We want to borrow a boat	more beautifully than English people.
If the weather is warm,	and I want to climb the highest one.

One oder *ones?*

7 Einkaufen. Schreibe *one* oder *ones* in die Lücken.

1. I like that painting. – Which __________?
2. Those shoes are nice. – Do you mean the green __________?
3. Let's buy some biscuits. – Yes, some chocolate __________.
4. How much is that cake, please? – That __________?

Fehlersuche

8 Besuch auf einen Bauernhof. Lies den Text und korrigiere die Fehler.

Last summer I stayed on a farm, ~~a beautiful~~ which had	→ *a beautiful one*
animals, and it was great. Life is very differently on	__________
a farm and I felt strange at first. The parents worked	__________
hardly every day and they didn't have much time to	__________
relax themselves, but life was well. They did almost	__________
everything theyselves. The mother made the bread,	__________
cheese and butter herself and it was the good food	__________
which I'd ever tasted. The children who school was	__________
miles away were the fittest children which I have ever	__________
met. They are my friends now and they visit us in the	__________
school holidays if their parents agree. I enjoyed me so	__________
much on the farm that I want to be a farmer now. It	__________
may be difficult but I'll learn even if I will have to teach	__________
everything.	__________

Zuhören und sich Notizen machen 24

9 Höre dir das Telefongespräch an. Notiere, was die Anruferin Ellis mitteilt: ihren Namen, ihre Mobiltelefonnummer und den Grund des Anrufs.

____

____

____

Sprechen: in einer Touristeninformation

10 Du bist mit deinem Vater in London. Er möchte ein Konzert besuchen, aber sein Englisch reicht nicht aus. Vermittle zwischen ihm und der Information.

Father: Ich würde gern wissen, ob es dieses Wochenende Chorkonzerte gibt.

You: ______________________________

Assistant: Let me see. Oh yes, there's a concert in Caerphilly this evening.

You: ______________________________

Father: Gibt es dazu Informationen?

You: ______________________________

Assistant: Yes, would you like some leaflets?

You: ______________________________

Father: Ja bitte. Und wie kommt man nach Caerphilly?

You: ______________________________

Assistant: You can get there by train.

You: ______________________________

Lesen und schreiben

11 Lies zunächst die E-Mail. Dann beantworte die Fragen dazu: *true, false* oder *not in the text?*

Hi Paul,
I've had a great week. The other people in my class are really nice and I've played football in the evening with them a few times. I've already joined a rap club and – don't laugh – a poetry club. And why did I join? You guessed it! I've met a girl who goes there. Sophie's great fun and beautiful, too. I've written a poem about her and I think it's quite good. There's a poetry slam next weekend and I'd like to read it out. But I'm not sure. Do you think it's a good idea? Will she laugh at me and never want to speak to me again? Or worse, will everybody in the class laugh at me? By the way, when do you want to come and visit me? Please write soon.
CU (or not)
Jake

1. Paul is in Jake's class. ________
2. Sophie goes to the poetry club. ________
3. Jake wants to read out a poem about Sophie at the poetry slam. ________
4. Jake wants to visit Paul. ________

12 Jetzt beantworte die E-Mail aus Aufgabe 11. Nimm die Notizen zu Hilfe.

glad – you enjoy yourself – if send poem – I read it – come next weekend? – like to meet Sophie and go to poetry slam

____
____
____
____
____
____
____

Unit 5

Kreuzworträtsel

1 Löse das Kreuzworträtsel und stelle aus den farbig hinterlegten Buchstaben das Lösungswort zusammen.

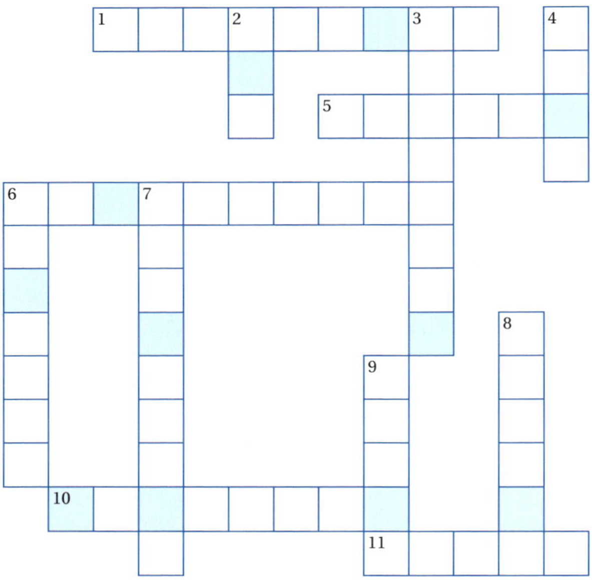

A piano and a recorder are both ____________.

across:

1. A lot of musicians play together in an …
5. When somebody sings in a band, you say they're on …
6. A … is the person who writes the lyrics
10. A … plays an instrument.
11. An … is like theatre where everybody sings.

down:

2. When a song is a …, you hear it on the radio a lot.
3. A … is often the first instrument a child plays.
4. A … guitar is almost like a normal guitar.
6. A … learns something.
7. A … plays a guitar.
8. A … is sombody who sings and talks.
9. If you play a …, you can usually play a keyboard, too.

Musik und mehr

2 Beschrifte die Bilder.

1. ______________

2. ______________

3. ______________

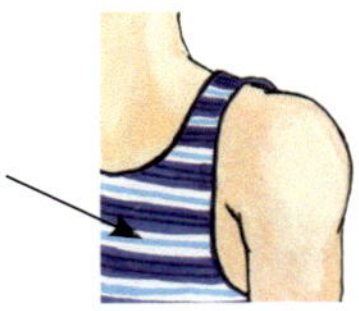

4. ______________

5. ______________

6. ______________

3 Auf Tournee. Löse die Buchstabenrätsel auf und ergänze die Wörter richtig.

strunsinemt – arecer – sicaclasl – taruig – ueque – cork – ettick ffoice – rout – cslyri

I love ______________ music – I love to try and hear the different ______________ which are playing in the orchestra. I also like reggae and ______________ and I was really glad to hear that U2, my favourite rock band, is going on ______________ next year and they are coming to my town. As soon as I heard they were coming I went to ______________ outside the ______________ – with hundreds of other people – and with my ______________. I know all the ______________ to Bono's songs, of course, and I played a few while I was waiting. The people around me liked it and that, I hope, was the start of my ______________ as a musician.

Adjektive

4 Ergänze die Adjektive richtig.

1. You weren't very polite. You were r _ _ _.
2. If you're mad, you could be crazy or you could just be a _ _ r _.
3. If you need a drink, then you're t _ _ _ _ _ _.
4. When you win lots of things, you're s _ _ _ _ _ _ f _ _.
5. People who are nice to other people are k _ _ _.
6. Something that you can do is p _ _ _ _ b l _.
7. Something that you would like to forget is e _ b _ _ _ _ _ _ _ _ g.
8. If you have not got enough money, then you are p _ _ _.

5 Wandle die Verben in Adjektive um und trage sie oder ihr Gegenteil in den richtigen Sätzen ein.

break – climb – eat – enjoy – play – read – solve

I don't like that game. It's ________________.

That book is terrible. It's ________________.

That's a special glass. It's ________________.

That was a great party. It was very ________________.

The police have problems with some mysteries. They are ________________.

That mountain isn't very high. It's ________________.

I made a cake but it was ________________.

Tipp Mithilfe von Präfixen und Suffixen kannst du sowohl neue Wörter bilden als auch unbekannte Wörter verstehen: *-able* bedeutet beispielsweise „-bar“: drinkable – trinkbar

A piece of . . .

6 Beschrifte die Bilder mit *a piece of* …

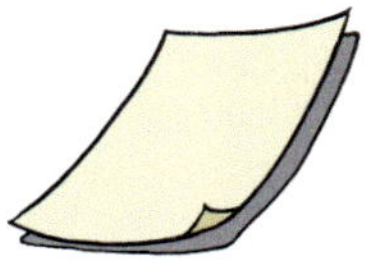

1. ______________________ 2. ______________________

3. ______________________ 4. two ______________________

Wichtige Wendungen: jemandem helfen/sich entschuldigen

7 Bilde aus den angegebenen Wörtern Sätze und trage sie richtig ein.

very/of/that's/you/kind **to/I/rude/didn't/be/mean** **help/you/can/I**

Man: Are you lost? ______________________?

Woman: Yes please. Can you tell me how to get to the waterfront museum?

Man: Yes, I can show you the way if you like.

Woman: ______________________.

Girl: I'm terrible sorry if I hurt you yesterday.

Girl: ______________________.

Wiederholung: die modalen Hilfsverben

Can, may, must, should und ihre Verneinungen ***can't, may not, mustn't, shouldn't*** und ***needn't*** sind modale Hilfsverben. Du kannst sie nur im *simple present* verwenden, mit der Ausnahme von *could*, das eine Vergangenheitsform ist.

Nach einem modalen Hilfsverb steht immer die Grundform des Verbs ohne *to*. Die Form der *modals* ist für alle Personen gleich.

She **can** speak French. She **couldn't** last year.	Sie kann Französisch (sprechen). … konnte sie es nicht. (Fähigkeit)
Can/May I have a cake?	Darf ich … haben? (Erlaubnis)
You **can't/mustn't** swim now.	Du darfst jetzt nicht … (Verbot)
I **must** call Jill quickly.	Ich muss schnell Jill anrufen. (notwendig)
You **should** eat less.	Du solltest weniger essen. (Rat)
I **needn't** go to bed yet.	Ich muss noch nicht ins Bett gehen. (nicht notwendig)
Can/Could/Will/Would you help me?	Könntest du mir helfen? (Bitte)

8 Ein Besuch im Globe Theatre. Übersetze die Sätze.

1. Ich kann die Schauspieler dort gut verstehen.

_______________________________ the actors there very well.

2. Wir müssen nicht die ganze Zeit auf unseren Plätzen sitzen.

_______________________________ in our seats all the time.

3. Du musst eine Eintrittskarte kaufen.

____

4. Wir dürfen keine Fotos machen.

____

Wiederholung: Fragen im Überblick

Bei Fragen stellt man immer ein Modalverb, ein Hilfsverb oder eine Form des Verbs *be* vor das Subjekt.

Fragen mit *do/does* und *did*:

Do they **live** here? **Does** she **like** this music?
Did you **go** to the concert?

Fragen mit dem Verb *to be:*

Are you good at singing?
Was he at the concert yesterday?

Fragen mit mehrteiligen Verbformen:

Can I **help** you?
Have you **been** to Paris?
Are you **listening** to me?
Would you **like** a drink?

Bei **Fragen mit Fragewörtern** stellt man das Fragewort immer voran:

Where are you going?
What did you do yesterday?
Who do you know?

Bestätigungsfragen:

You like that, **don't you?**
The concert wasn't very good, **was it?**

9 Ein Konzert. Formuliere mithilfe der angegebenen Wörter Fragen in der einfachen Gegenwart.

how much – be – tickets – please – ?

____

what time – the concert – start – ?

____

I – can – buy – two tickets – please – ?

____

10 Ein Interview mit einem Musiker. Ergänze Fragen, die zu den Antworten passen. Tipp: Die Aussage, nach der du fragen sollst, ist farbig markiert.

1. ______________________________

I've sold two million singles.

2. ______________________________

I'm going to make my next CD in July.

3. ______________________________

I can play the guitar, bass and the piano.

4. ______________________________

I practise every day.

5. ______________________________

Yes, I was good at music when I was a child.

6. ______________________________

Last weekend I relaxed at home with my family.

11 Ergänze die Sätze mit dem richtigen *question tag*.

You like music, ______________?

John can't sing at all, ______________?

You haven't got the new CD already, ______________?

Beyoncé has played here a few times, ______________?

He had problems with drugs, ______________?

Fragen mit dem modalen Hilfsverb *shall*

Mit ***Shall I ...?*** und ***Shall we ...?*** kann man jemandem etwas anbieten oder vorschlagen:
Shall I get you a sandwich? – Soll ich dir ein Sandwich holden?
Shall I look after them for you? – Soll ich für dich auf sie aufpassen?
Shall we go to the concert? – Sollen wir zu dem Konzert gehen?

12 Lies die Situationen durch, dann biete den jeweiligen Personen etwas an. Verwende dazu *shall* und das angegebene Verb.

An old woman is carrying very heavy bags.

→ carry: Shall ______________________________?

Your English grandma has arrived at your house. She likes cups of tea.

→ make: ______________________________

Your friend wants to hear the new song you have written.

→ sing: ______________________________

13 Verbinde die Sätze jeweils mit dem passenden Vorschlag.

There's good film on at the cinema.	Shall we get the bus home?
You want to sing a new song with your band.	Shall we go and watch it?
You're hungry.	Shall we write one?
You're tired.	Shall we buy a sandwich?

Die modalen Hilfsverben und ihre Ersatzformen

Weil man die modalen Hilfsverben nur im *present tense* verwenden kann, benutzt man in den anderen Zeiten die Ersatzformen ***be able to, be allowed to*** und ***have to.***

can (not) → to (not) be able to *([nicht] können):*
Many people **are able to/can play** an instrument. *(present)*
We **couldn't/weren't able to play** one two years ago. *(past)*

can/may → to be allowed to *(dürfen):*
May/Can/Am I **allowed to take** a photo? *(present)*
We **were allowed to talk** to the band later. *(past)*

can't/may not/mustn't → to not be allowed to *(nicht dürfen):*
You **mustn't/can't/may not talk** loudly in a library. *(present)*
We **weren't allowed to eat** at the concert. *(past)*

must → to have to *(müssen:)*
We **must/have to learn** French. *(present)*
My brother **had to learn** Spanish, too. *(past)*

needn't – don't have to *(nicht müssen):*
I **needn't/don't have to get up** before eight. *(present)*
I **didn't have to go** to bed early last weekend. *(past)*

14 Formuliere diese Sätze neu, indem du ein Modalverb verwendest.

Jenny is not able to remember the lyrics.

____

David doesn't have to sing.

____

They all have to practise a lot.

____

John isn't allowed to practise the drums at home.

____

15 Ein Besuch in London. Welcher Satz aus der Auswahl ist bedeutungsgleich? Nenne den Buchstaben.

1. We mustn't drive on the right. → ____________
a) We aren't able to drive on the right.
b) We aren't allowed to drive on the right.
c) We don't have to drive on the right.

2. May I go to the cinema? → ____________
a) Am I allowed to go to the cinema?
b) Do I have to go to the cinema?
c) Am I able to go to the cinema?

3. We needn't walk everywhere. → ____________
a) We aren't able to walk everywhere.
b) We aren't allowed to walk everywhere.
c) We don't have to walk everywhere.

16 Eine Musikerin. Lies, was in den Denkblasen steht, dann gib die Sätze mit Hilfe von Ersatzformen so wieder, wie sie sie heute formulieren würde.

1. When I was five, I ____.

2. I ______________________________ when my parents listened to music.

3. ____

4. ____

5. ____

Die Ersatzformen in verschiedenen Zeiten: Überblick

Man kann die Ersatzverben ***be able to, be allowed to*** and ***have to*** in allen Zeiten verwenden:

	simple past	***present perfect***	***will future***
can	was/were able to	has/have been able to	will be able to
may	was/were allowed to	has/have been allowed to	will be allowed to
must	had to	has/have had to	will have to
needn't	didn't have to	hasn't/haven't had to	won't have to
mustn't/ may not	wasn't/weren't allowed to	hasn't/haven't been allowed to	won't be allowed to

17 Urlaub in England. John und Sarah aus den USA erzählen. Setze die passenden Ersatzverben im *present perfect* ein.

We've had a great holiday and lots of things have been different. Usually when we buy things in the shops, we needn't think too hard but here we ____________________ try hard to understand people. Usually we can understand everything on TV but we ________________________ in England. Usually we must go to bed early but on holiday we ____________________ go to bed before 11 pm. And usually we can't get up late – our mother doesn't let us stay in bed after 7 am – but on holiday we ________________________ stay in bed until lunchtime. But on holiday we've wanted to get up early.

Tipp

Mustn't und *needn't* werden leicht verwechselt. Hier kannst du Fehler vermeiden, wenn du dich an die Ersatzformen hältst!

18 Mary träumt von der Zeit, wenn sie endlich erwachsen sein wird. Übersetze.

Ich werde nach Hause kommen können, wann ich möchte.

______________________________ when I want to.

Ich werde das Essen kochen dürfen, das ich auch essen möchte.

______________________________ the food which I want to eat.

Aber vielleicht werde ich es nicht kochen können?

But maybe ______________________________ it?

Ich werde keine Hausaufgaben machen müssen, aber ich werde arbeiten müssen.

____

Ich werde nicht mehr in die Schule gehen dürfen. Schade!

______________________________ *any more.* What a pity!

19 Eine Opersängerin. Schreibe ganze Sätze und verwende die Ersatzform in der richtigen Zeit.

when – I – be – a child – I – can *(können)* – sing – very loudly

____

I – never – needn't – use – a microphone – to fill a concert hall

____

I – hope – I – may – sing – in operas – when – I – be – 70

____

Konjunktionen

Mit **Konjunktionen** verbindest du Sätze oder Satzteile miteinander:

after	I went home after the concert had finished.
although	I went to the concert although I don't like their music.
and	I play the drums and I can sing.
because	I can't have a piano because we haven't got room.
but	I like their music but I don't like their latest single.
or	You can buy a CD or download the music.
so	I read the lyrics so I can sing to the music.
while	We met while we were waiting for tickets.
as long as	As long as you practise enough, you'll learn.
as soon as	I'll practise again as soon as I have time.
before	I'll practise before I go to my next lesson.
if	If *(wenn)* I find a band, I'll join it. She wants to know if *(ob)* there's a concert tonight.
that	He told her that there isn't a concert this week.
until (till)	I'll practise until I'm the best.
when	I go to bed when I'm tired.

20 Ein Konzert. Ergänze den Text mit den richtigen Konjunktionen.

I meet my friend, Alan, __________ I am waiting for the bus into town. He tells me __________ there is a concert outside in the park this afternoon. He asks me __________ I want to go, too. It is a band that I don't like __________ I want to go __________ I like concerts – and Alan. I'll go __________ it's not too expensive.

It's 1 pm and the concert doesn't start __________ four. We decide to buy tickets first. __________ we've bought them, we go to a café in town __________ buy a drink. __________ we finish our drinks, it's 3 pm, ___ we walk slowly to the park. __________ we get there it starts to rain, __________ it doesn't matter; it's the best concert I've ever been to.

Lesen: Artikel über drei Bands

21 „Skimme“ die Lexikonartikel, dann kreuze die richtige Aussage an.

Bob Geldof is a singer, songwriter, actor and guitarist who became famous with the Boomtown Rats in the middle of the 1970s. The Boomtown Rats were an Irish band who played a mixture of punk and pop music and were successful mostly in Great Britain and Canada. Geldof himself became famous all over the world when he started Band Aid in 1984. Band Aid was a group of very famous musicians who made a record called, “Do they know it's Christmas?” They gave all the money to charity. The money went mostly to poor and hungry children in Africa. The next summer he organized the concert Live Aid. Live Aid took place in New York and London at the same time. It was one of the most famous concerts ever and all the money from the concert went to charity. Bob Geldof still works for Africa today.

The Rolling Stones is an English rock band that started in the 1960s with Mick Jagger on vocals, pianist Ian Stewart, guitarists Keith Richards and Brian Jones, bassist Bill Wyman and drummer Charlie Watts. The first leader of the band was Brian Jones but because Mick Jagger and Keith Richards wrote most of the songs, they became leaders soon after. The Rolling Stones first became famous in Great Britain but soon after became successful in the USA. The band has made over 20 albums and sold more than 200 million in the whole world. Their most famous single was “Satisfaction” and although not all the members of the band are the same, the Rolling Stones still go on tour.

Boney M. started in Germany in the 1970s as a disco and pop band. Frank Farian, who was already quite successful as a singer, sang most of the vocals himself for the band's first records. He went into the studio and changed his voice electronically so that he could sing the high and the low parts of the songs. He then put the parts together, again electronically, so that it sounded like a band. Later he found people to go on stage for him and move their lips to the music. This was quite normal at the time so there was no scandal. The other members of the band changed often at the beginning but at the end the band members were Maizie Williams, Marcia Barrett, Liz Mitchell and Bobby Farrell. Maizie and Bobby, who was an exotic dancer, didn't sing on the records but they did sing on stage. You can still buy Boney M. records today but usually only one of the original four sing in them together with new singers.

1. They all still play. ☐
2. They all play the same kind of music. ☐
3. They are all bands. ☐
4. They are all British. ☐

22 Jetzt „scanne“ die Artikel. Wie lauten die gesuchten Begriffe?

1. a band which plays punk ____________________
2. an Irish man ____________________
3. a German man ____________________
4. a band which plays rock ____________________
5. a band which plays disco music ____________________
6. a man who made lots of money for poor people ____________________
7. singers who do not sing ____________________

23 Trage die geeigneten Konjunktionen ein.

after – although – but – before – because – but – while – because

1. _______________ Geldof played with a successful band, he became really famous when he started Band Aid. _______________ Geldof had been successful with Band Aid, he organized Live Aid. Live Aid was very famous _______________ it took place in New York and London at the same time.

2. Mick Jagger and Keith Richards became leaders of the Rolling Stones _______________ they wrote most of the songs. _______________ the Rolling Stones became famous in the States, they were successful in Great Britain. You can still see the Rolling Stones _______________ without some of their first members.

3. _______________ Frank Farian was working as a singer himself, he started his new band Boney M. He sang at least two voices in the songs _______________ other people went on stage for him.

Zuhören: Aussprache 25

24 Lies dir erst die Wörter durch, dann höre dir die CD an. Welches Wort wird gesprochen?

1. her	☐	hear	☐
2. door	☐	tour	☐
3. jazz	☐	chess	☐
4. vest	☐	west	☐
5. live	☐	life	☐

Zuhören und richtig reagieren 26

25 Du hörst drei Kurzdialoge, in denen jeweils eine Zeile ausgelassen ist *(part 1)*. Welche Zeile fehlt? Wähle die beste Antwort. Höre dann *part 2* der Lösung an und prüfe, ob du Recht hattest.

1. a) You've been a great help. ☐
   b) That's very kind of you. Thanks. ☐
   c) Don't worry. ☐
2. a) Shall I open that door for you? ☐
   b) Can I open that door for you? ☐
   c) Could you open that door for me, please? ☐
3. a) Don't worry. ☐
   b) I didn't mean to be rude. ☐
   c) That's very kind of you. ☐

Zuhören: eine Band in der Klemme 27

26 Höre dir den Dialog zwischen Jenny und Pete an. Lies die Fragen und kreuze die richtigen Antworten an.

1. Who is Joey? → ______
a) He's a singer in Pete's band.
b) He's a guitarist in Pete's band.
c) He's the songwriter.

2. When's their concert? → ______
a) On Friday.
b) On Saturday.
c) On Sunday.

3. Why is Pete unhappy? → ______
a) Joey does not want to sing.
b) Joey may not sing on Saturday.
c) Joey can't sing on Saturday.

4. Can Jenny sing well? → ______
a) Yes, but she's too nervous.
b) Yes, but she doesn't like it.
c) No, she can't.

5. What are they going to sing? → ______
a) Famous songs.
b) Their own songs.
c) Famous songs and their own.

6. What does Jenny decide? → ______
a) She wants to sing with them.
b) She doesn't want to sing.
c) She wants to watch the concert.

27 Höre dir CD-Track 27 nochmals an. Wer sagt die Sätze: Jenny oder Pete?

1. It's our first one and we really wanted to play. ______________
2. Will you help us then? ______________
3. I'll go and get the lyrics now. ______________
4. I didn't know that you wrote your own songs. ______________
5. They aren't rude, are they? ______________

28 Verbinde diese Satzteile aus dem Dialog zu ganzen Sätzen.

I won't be able to	close your eyes and imagine you're in the bathroom.
You'll just have to	learn so many songs before Saturday, will I?
We aren't allowed to	sing in front of lots of people.
I won't be able to	sing them at school.

Skills workshop 5

Writing skills

Je nachdem, was man schreibt, verwendet man einen anderen Stil.

Tagebuch: Hier kannst du so schreiben, wie du willst, weil der Inhalt nur für dich bestimmt ist. Egal ob du dir nur Notizen machst oder seitenlange Berichte verfasst, alles ist erlaubt.

SMS: Weil es hier meist darum geht, schnell zu schreiben, kannst du dich kurz fassen und Abkürzungen (auch selbst erfundene) oder Zahlen statt Worte verwenden, z. B. *2morrow.* Achte aber darauf, dass deine Nachricht noch verständlich ist.

Notizen: Vergiss nicht den Adressaten deiner Notiz. Stichpunkte oder kurze Sätze sind hier völlig ausreichend.

Gedichte, Reime oder ein Rap: Hier geht es darum, dass es sich „gut liest". Mit dieser Textsorte kannst du komplexe Ideen oder tiefe Gefühle mit wenigen Worten ausdrücken.

E-Mails oder Briefe: Vor allem Briefe sind normalerweise länger als SMS oder Notizen. Du benutzt hier ganze Sätze, aber der Stil hängt auch davon ab, ob du einen privaten oder eher formellen Brief schreibst. Ein Brief hat einen festen Aufbau:

1. Die Absenderadresse steht oben.
2. Unter der Adresse folgt das Datum.
3. Fange mit „Dear" und dem Namen des Empfängers an.
4. Teile dem Adressaten mit, aus welchem Grund du schreibst.
5. Verwende für einen neuen Gedanken auch einen neuen Absatz.
6. Verabschiede dich, z. B. mit *Best wishes*, *Yours* oder *Love*.
7. Unterschreibe mit deinem Namen.

1 Lies die folgenden Texte. Um welche Art von Texten handelt es sich?

A

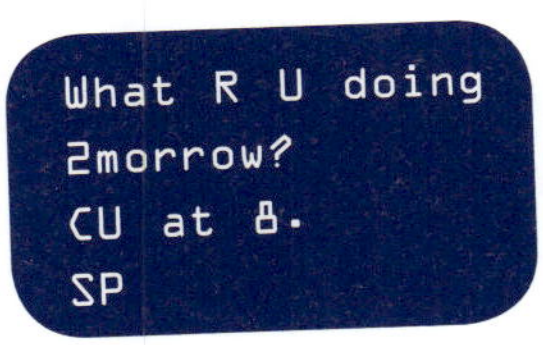

B

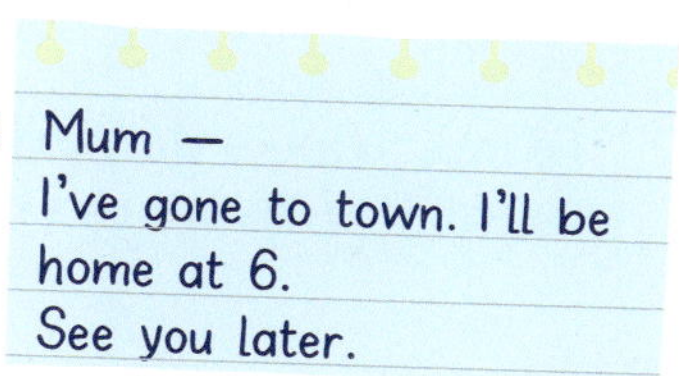

C Saturday
What a terrible week! Homework, tests, homework, tests. I'm glad we're on holiday this week. What shall I do now? Phone Jane? Maybe later. I'm so tired, I think I'll go back to bed.

D Dear Jim,
How are things in Brighton? Do you like your new school? I've had a bad week. School was terrible. My parents have argued all week. And I miss you. Please phone this evening.
Love
Jane

E I feel fine
I'm on cloud nine
'Cos you are mine

A: ______________ B: ______________ C: ______________

D: ______________ E: ______________

2 Steffen schreibt einen Brief an einen Freund in England, Daniel. Lies ihn und bringe die Abschnitte in die richtige Reihenfolge.

A	How are you? We're all well and I'm writing to ask if we can come and visit you in London in the summer. I decided to write because on the phone I often say something wrong.
B	10th May
C	Dear Daniel,
D	Kirchgasse 15 70183 Stuttgart
E	Mum, Dad, me and Chris are all going to travel around England and maybe Austria this summer and we would love to come and visit you, too. We haven't planned everything yet but we think that we'll be in south England in August. When do you think is the best time to visit? Can you suggest any hotels in the area where we could stay? What can we do in the area? Is there anything we shouldn't miss?
F	Best wishes,
G	Steffen
H	I'd love to meet you again. Do you still go skiing in the winter? It was a great holiday which we went on last year, wasn't it?

1. ______ 2. ______ 3. ______ 4. ______ 5. ______ 6. ______ 7. ______ 8. ______

3 Übernimm nun die Rolle von Daniel: Verwende die angegebenen Informationen, um den Brief zu beantworten. Ordne die Informationen in Absätze und beginne und beende den Brief richtig.

- thank him for his letter
- you would love to see him in London
- doesn't need a hotel – enough room at your house
- best time to come – at the end of August
- shouldn't miss – Notting Hill Carnival or Science Museum
- stay for two weeks!
- skiing holiday was great – haven't been since – wants to go again

Test practice C

Your summer holidays

This week Mark from Year 10 has written about his holidays in Manchester.

M is for Mad, Manchester and Music

Holidays in Manchester? Sounds strange? Well, it was great; my best ever holiday – and no, not because I met my new girlfriend there! (Sorry, Lucy!) OK. It's true that I wasn't excited about it before I went. When my dad told us that we had to spend a week in Manchester at my cousin's house for our summer holidays, I just thought, "Oh no." I've got nothing against my cousins, of course, but who wants to go to Manchester when you live in beautiful Bristol? I could only think of industry, factories, rain and football, and as my friends all know, I'm not a football fan.

So what did I like about it? It's exciting and there's so much you can do there. It's great for live music. You can hear almost any kind you want. And there's new bands playing all the time. Who knows? Maybe I have already seen the new Robbie Williams! (OK, I know that he wasn't born in Manchester but he started his career there with Take That.) There were lots of festivals there in the summer inside and outside – often the music was so good that we didn't even notice that it was raining – again. When we'd seen lots in the city of Manchester, we took the bus to Didsbury. Lots of students live there and there's lots more to do here – more music, more pubs and more cafés.

The other great thing about Manchester is that there are lots of fun places you can visit that aren't far away. If the weather's good, you can go to Blackpool, for example. It's the most popular holiday seaside town in the UK. It has a very long sandy beach which is good because there is something for everybody. You can ride on ponies, listen to music or watch beach theatre. There are also three piers, Blackpool Tower and the Pleasure Beach, which is a giant theme park with a great ghost train.

If you go east from Manchester, you can visit Edale. Edale is a small village in the middle of the Pennines. That are the mountains which run down the middle of England. It is a beautiful area and it's great for sports. You can walk, climb, ride horses or go camping or mountain-biking.

Reading

1 Welche dieser Dinge verband Mark mit Manchester, bevor er dort war, und an welche denkt er danach?

factories – festivals – football – industry – interesting places – music – rain – students

before: ____________________

after: ____________________

2 Was kannst du an diesen Orten unternehmen?

Didsbury: ____________________

Blackpool: ____________________

____

Edale: ____________________

____

3 Kreuze die richtige Antwort an.

1. Mark is from	a) Blackpool	☐.	b) Bristol	☐.	c) Manchester	☐.
2. Mark likes	a) football	☐.	b) music	☐.	c) rain	☐.
3. Robbie Williams	a) was born	☐	b) sang	☐	c) died in Manchester.	☐
4. The Pleasure Beach is	a) a beach	☐.	b) a pier	☐.	c) a theme park	☐.
5. The Pennines are	a) mountains	☐.	b) a village	☐.	c) in Manchester	☐.

Language

4 Was bedeuten diese Wörter? Denke an ähnliche deutsche oder englische Wörter.

fun (line 19): ______________ theme park (line 25): ______________

seaside (line 21): ______________

ponies (line 23): ______________

5 *That* kann Relativpronomen („der/die/das"), Demonstrativpronomen („das") oder Konjunktion („dass") sein. Welche Bedeutung hat es an diesen Textstellen?

1. (line 4): ______________ 4. (line 20): ______________

2. (line 13): ______________ 5. (line 27): ______________

3. (line 15): ______________

Passing on information

6 Du bist mit deinen Eltern in Manchester. Ihr möchtet ein Klassikkonzert besuchen. Vermittle für deine Eltern.

Father: Gibt es besondere Preise für Kinder oder Familien?

You: ______________________________

Assistant: Yes, it's half the price for children under sixteen.

You: ______________________________

Mother: Frag ihn, ob wir Fotos machen dürfen.

You: ______________________________

Assistant: No, you can't but you can buy photos in the shop.

You: ______________________________

Listening 28

7 In der Touristeninformation von Manchester. Höre dir den Dialog auf der CD an und beantworte danach die Fragen.

1. Who says: "We'd like to see some of the area around Manchester"? ______________
2. Who says: "Where would you like to go most?" ______________
3. Where does the man want to go? ______________
4. What is Southport like? ______________
5. Where can he get train tickets? ______________

Writing

8 Schreibe mithilfe der Notizen einen Text über Tübingen. Verwende Relativsätze und Konjunktionen!

- student town
- winter – Christmas market/skiing in Swabian Alb
- Swabian Alb – mountains near the town
- summer – boats on river/walk or cycle in country
- country around town is beautiful
- all year – music, food and film festivals

____

____

____

____

____

____

____

____

____

Unit 1

1 1. football: a) goal post, b) goal, c) goalkeeper
2. tennis: a) racket, b) net
3. swimming: a) swimming cap, b) goggles
4. rugby: a) pitch

2 1. referee; 2. surfer; 3. star; 4. coach; 5. loser; 6. scorer

3 I'm City's best fan. I always go to the matches and get there early. Today we're playing Brighton but I don't like them. They always play hard and they never **play fairly.** When they **tackle,** they always go for the knees and not for the ball. In fact I often think they **kick** our players more often than they get the ball. When the referee isn't looking, they often **hit** our best players, too, and then we need to **substitute** them before they are tired. Our players are often too scared to **score** a goal or even to go near the net – and that's just while they are warming up.

4 spare – extra; chat – talk; article – thing; arrangement – plan; nil – zero

5

c	**o**	**m**	**p**	**l**	**a**	**i**	**n**	e
s	**r**	**e**	**p**	**o**	**r**	**t**	t	h
f	n	h	d	g	**r**	a	u	q
q	d	m	v	**m**	**a**	**t**	**c**	**h**
o	v	**s**	**o**	**u**	**n**	**d**	h	**b**
b	**f**	a	i	m	**g**	n	y	**r**
b	**e**	**c**	**o**	**m**	**e**	u	w	**e**
l	**e**	r	k	z	z	k	p	**a**
c	**l**	x	j	**t**	**h**	**a**	**n**	**k**

werden – to become;
verabreden – to arrange;
klingen – to sound;
sich fühlen – to feel;
passen – to match;
sich beschweren – to complain;
kaputtmachen – to break;
sich bedanken – to thank;
berichten – to report

6 feeling – Gefühl: to feel – fühlen
to agree – zustimmen: disagree – widersprechen
lonely – einsam: alone

tradition – Tradition: *frz.* la tradition
tiring – ermüdend: tired – müde
home-made – hausgemacht: home *und* made
happily – glücklich(erweise) *(Adverb):* happy – glücklich
hot chocolate – heiße Schokolade: hot *and* chocolate
foggy – neblig: fog – Nebel

7 **Age:** 14
Height: 5 feet 8 **inches (5' 8")**
Weight: 8 **stone** 5 pounds
Birthday: 7th July
Likes: swimming, **rugby**

8 What's the name **of** your favourite tennis player? Mine is Andy Murray. I've seen him play tennis **on** TV a few times and I even saw him **in** a shop **in** London once. But next week **on** Saturday I'm going to watch him play **at** Wimbledon. The game starts **at** 3 o'clock **in** the afternoon and I'm really looking forward to it. I'm going with a friend **from** my tennis club and I hope it doesn't rain. Not that it ever rains **in** London, of course!

9 **agreeing and disagreeing:** Sorry, I think you're wrong/That's what I think, too./I know what you mean.
arranging to meet: Have you got anything planned on Wednesday?/What are you doing at the weekend?/Sorry, I've got other plans.

10 Which sport do you like best? – Table tennis.
Are you good at table tennis? – No, I'm not.
Do you want to play now? – Yes, I do.
Have you got a ball? – No, I haven't.
Does Jim have a ball? – Yes, he does.

11 How often do you train?
I train three times a week.
Are your parents good at sport?
Yes, they are. My dad is very good at tennis, too.
Does your father help you?
Yes, he often practises with me.

12 I **like** Ann and I **love** football but I **don't have** time for both. So what can I do? **Does Ann play** football? No, **she doesn't,** but she **plays** hockey. I **don't play** hockey but I **have** an idea. Ann's friend, Sophie, **plays** football. And **is she** nice, too? Yes, she is.

13
1. What **are they doing** now? They **aren't playing tennis.** They **are jogging.**
2. What **is she doing** at the moment? She **isn't playing rugby.** She **is playing basketball.**
3. **Are the fish playing** tennis? **No, they aren't. They are playing volleyball.**
4. Is the boy walking? No, he isn't. He's riding his bike.

14
John: Hi Gemma. How **is it going** now?
Gemma: Oh, fine. We**'re just having** a picnic.
John: No, I mean in the game. **Are they playing** well?
Gemma: Oh, the game! I don't know. I **don't understand** it at all. The man **hits** the ball and then sometimes he **runs** and scores but sometimes he **doesn't run** at all and he scores even more.
John: Oh, Gemma. **Do you know** the rules?
Gemma: Of course not. Girls **don't play** cricket at school.
John: So why did you go?
Gemma: Well, my brother bought the tickets and the picnic and I **love** picnics.

15
It's Saturday morning and I**'m sitting** in bed at home. I**'m reading** a book and I**'m listening** to music. My parents **are having** breakfast downstairs. I can hear them. On Saturday I usually **get up** early and **go jogging.** Then I **have** breakfast and then I **go** to football training. I**'m staying** at home today because I'm ill. And I **like** it. I think I'll stay at home next week, too.

16
Jake: Look! The/That girl is doing a super/great trick.
Ruth: Yes, she often wins.
Jake: And what is Jean doing at the moment/now?
Ruth: She's waiting and listening to music.
Jake: Why isn't she watching?
Ruth: She never watches. It makes her nervous.

17
You often go to the skateboard park, don't you?
You don't like the park in town, do you?
That's your new skateboard, isn't it?
That trick isn't easy, is it?
John has a new skateboard, doesn't he?
He's already won a competition on it, hasn't he?
But he doesn't practise very often, does he?
He hasn't taught you his new trick, has he?
You can't do it already, can you?

18
Tom: You haven't been here before, **have you?**
Alice: No, I haven't. And you know everybody here, **don't you?**

Tom: Yes, almost. I like it here. There are lots of things to do here, **aren't there?**
Alice: Yes. Look! They're good at basketball, **aren't they?**
Tom: Yes, they haven't made any silly mistakes, **have they?**
Alice: No, they haven't. And you can play well, too, **can't you?**
Tom: Yes, but how do you know? Oh. You've just started at my school, **haven't you?** And my friend, Mark, told you about this youth club, **didn't he?**
Alice: Yes, he did. But he isn't here today, **is he?**
Tom: No, he's ill. So we can play badminton together, **can't we?**

19

1. You can't play tennis well, **can you?** – Yes, I can.
2. You've been to Wimbledon, **haven't you?** – Yes, I have.
3. Andy often wins matches, **doesn't he?** – Yes, he does.
4. They're playing well, **aren't they?** – Yes, they are.

20

What are you doing at the weekend?
I'm playing tennis on Saturday.
Pete is skateboarding on Sunday.
We are watching cricket/the cricket.

21

1.
Boy: I'm going to a hockey match tomorrow evening. What are you doing?
Girl: I'm meeting Tina.
2.
Girl: Where's Chris?
Boy: He's at the tennis club. He's playing tennis with some mates.
3.
Boy: You're in a hurry. Where are you going?
Girl: I'm going to the skatepark. Do you want to come?
Boy: No, some friends are coming to my house at 8 pm.

1. a) future, b) future; 2. present; 3. a) present, b) present, c) future

22

Tim: **Are you going** to Brighton for the marathon tomorrow?
Mike: Yes, **I am. I'm going** by bus. **Do you want** to come with me?
Tim: I **don't know.** I don't like marathons really. But I like the sea. What time **are you going?**
Mike: We**'re leaving** about 12.30.
Tim: That's very early.
Mike: Yes, but I**'m meeting** Pete at one so we can warm up first.
Tim: Why **do you want** to warm up first?
Mike: Didn't you know? We**'re running** in the marathon.

23 1. cricket; 2. tennis; 3. hockey

24 1. 11; 2. white; 3. English-speaking countries; 4. a racket and a ball; 5. in England and Wales (an earlier version started in France); 6. 4000 years old; 7. on a grass pitch

25 Text 1: This game is slow but it isn't easy/is hard to understand.
Text 2: People played a kind of this game earlier in France.
Text 3: People all over the world play this game.

26

Radio interviewer:	Hello, David. It's nice to have you here.
David:	Thanks.
Radio interviewer:	Let me just check my information is right. Now your full name is David Michael Roberts?
David:	Yes, that's right.
Radio interviewer:	And you're fifteen years old and the best hockey player in Birmingham.
David:	Well, yes, I'm 15 and I'm good at hockey.
Radio interviewer:	You're almost six foot, I think. Does that help in hockey matches?
David:	It's true, I'm five feet ten inches and most players are smaller than me but I don't know if it really helps. It's not basketball. But I only weigh eight stone fifteen and maybe that helps me to run faster.
Radio interviewer:	Eight stone fifteen? Yes, that's not much. Don't you like food?
David:	Oh yes, I love food, but I train almost every day so I don't weigh a lot.
Radio interviewer:	So you like food and hockey. What don't you like?
David:	Hm. I don't like tests at school. And I don't like hot chocolate.

Full name: David Michael Roberts
Age: **15**
Height: **five feet, ten inches (5' 10")**
Weight: **eight stone, fifteen pounds**
Birthday: **13th June**
Likes: **hockey, food**
Doesn't like: **tests, hot chocolate**

27 [g]: ru**g**by, fo**g**
[k]: **k**i**ck**, s**c**ore, be**c**ome
[l]: fou**l**, tack**l**e, comp**l**ain
[s]: **s**tone, **s**ound
[t]: ne**t**, **t**iring, cha**t**

28 *Ann:* Oh, Sally, I don't understand it. Why can't girls play football at our school? It isn't fair.
Sally: But, Ann, no other girls want to play football.
Ann: That's not true. I know lots of other girls who want to play football.
Sally: OK. Well, most girls don't want to play football. Football's hard and dangerous – just like boys.
Ann: Rubbish. Hockey's much harder than football and we have to play that. I hate it. There's always some girl who hits my legs with her stick – and that hurts much more than someone's foot.
Sally: That's because you're so fast. That's the only way the other players can stop you.
Ann: Oh, don't be silly. Sometimes players want to stop me, but most of the time they just run the wrong way. Susan even hit me on the head with her stick once. But anyway football's just so much more fun than hockey.
Sally: Yes, I agree with you. It's much more fun to watch when men play it. They always have great legs.
Ann: Oh, Sally. You're boy mad.
Sally: And women just aren't as good as men. They haven't got the skill.
Ann: Yes, you're right. And why? Because most girls can't play it at school.
Sally: Well, why don't you ask one of the sports teachers if you can start a team? I'm sure they'll help you. Then you can put some signs on the walls around school and see how many girls are interested.
Ann: That's a good idea. I'm going to hockey training at six o'clock so I can ask Mr Simon. Do you want to come with me?
Sally: Yes, OK. He's really nice.
Ann: Oh, Sally. He's a teacher.

1. **c)** passt am besten.
2. But, Ann, no other girls want to play football. – That's not true.
Football's hard and dangerous. – Rubbish.
That's the only way the other players can stop you. – Oh, don't be silly.
... football's just so much more fun than hockey. – Yes, I agree with you.
They haven't got the skill. – Yes, you're right.
3. a) false; b) true; c) true; d) true; e) false; *Korrektur:* a) Ann thinks that hockey is more dangerous than football. e) Sally has the idea to start a football team.

Skills workshop 1

1 1. A; 2. C; 3. B; 4. A/B; 5. C; 6. B; 7. A/B; 8. A; 9. B/C

2 **start of talk:** We're going to tell you .../First I'd like to tell you ...
middle of talk: As you can see in the picture .../Next ...
end of talk: Are there any questions?/Thank you for listening.
asking questions: Can you explain why ...?/Do you know who ...?
(not) answering questions: I'm not sure but I think .../Sorry, but I don't know.

3 Good morning everyone. Today **we're going to tell you** about the history of football. Now everybody believes that football started in England but did it really? This is the question which we are now going to answer.
First I'd like to tell you something about the history of sport. We're going to travel back in time. You have to imagine that we're now living at a time when life is getting easier for people. People don't have to work all the time so that they can have enough to eat. They now have some free time. So they make music, they tell stories, they draw pictures and they want to play games. So they run, they throw things. They make balls because they are easy to catch and then they start to kick them. This happens all over the world – everywhere that life is easy enough.
At first the games didn't have any rules. In the eleventh and twelfth centuries in England, villages played against each other. **As you can see in this picture,** they didn't just kick the ball. They threw, kicked and carried it. So many people played that the kings tried to stop the game. They wanted people to practise for battles.
Everybody played the game at first but from about the nineteenth century workers had less time to play football because they had to work so much. Now many pupils at expensive schools played the game. The pupils and the head teachers at these schools were some of the first people to write rules. The world's oldest clubs were at English schools. So to answer our first question: yes, the game of modern football probably started in England.
Thank you for listening. Are there any questions?

Phrases: 2, 3, 5, 6, 8

4 1. That was inter**esting.**
2. I under**stood** every**thing.**
3. You spoke very cl**early.**
4. I really enj**oyed** that.

Test practice A

1 1. D; 2. A; 3. C; 4. B

2 1. Ann; 2. Christine; 3. Sally

3 1. c); 2. a); 3. b); 4. a); 5. c); 6. a)

4 1. present; 2. future; 3. past; 4. future; 5. present; 6. past

5
Cousin: When are you practising next?
You: **Meine Cousine möchte wissen, wann ihr das nächste Mal übt.**
Captain: Wir trainieren am Freitagnachmittag. Möchtest du mit uns spielen?
You: **They're training on Friday afternoon. Would you like to play with them?**
Cousin: Yes, please. See you on Friday.
You: **Ja, würde sie gern. Sie kommt dann am Freitag.**

6
Jane: Do you want to play tennis at the weekend?
Ellis: Yes, why not. What about Saturday morning?
Jane: No, I'm sorry. I always go swimming on Saturday morning. Are you busy in the afternoon?
Ellis: Yes, I am. I'm watching the hockey match at school.
Jane: Oh, I wanted to watch that.
Ellis: Well, why don't you come, too?
Jane: What time does it start?
Ellis: It starts at three. We could meet at two forty-five at school.
Jane: Yes, OK. See you then.

When: Saturday; 2:45; Where: school; What: hockey match

7 Ann's full name is Ann Jane Ellis and she's fourteen years old. She likes all sport and hip hop music. She doesn't like rice or History homework.

Unit 2

1 1. fortress; 2. prison; 3. palace; 4. theatre

2 Last weekend I went on my first trip to London. Of course, I wanted to see all the famous **landmarks** so I went to Buckingham Palace first. I hoped to see the **royal family** there but I think they were on holiday at one of their palaces in Scotland. I went on a tour of the **building** anyway and it was interesting to see all the old and expensive **paintings** on the wall. Then I went on the London Eye which is a big **Ferris wheel** on the River Thames. You get a great view from there.
But the very best part of my trip came at the end. We went to the Notting Hill Carnival and watched the **parade** there. We ate delicious food and danced in the streets. Yes, it was brilliant.

3 1. hotel; 2. university; 3. palace; 4. cathedral; 5. market; 6. theatre

4 Could you help me, please?
How do I get to Covent Garden Market, please?
Take the Central Line westbound.
Change at Holborn after three stops.
Change to the Piccadilly Line southbound.
Get off at Covent Garden.

5 1. scientist; 2. detective; 3. chef; 4. hairdresser; 5. servant; 6. courier

6 1. teena**g**er**s**; 2. nep**h**ew; 3. **a**rchitect; 4. neigh**b**our; 5. heir; 6. **a**ssista**n**t; 7. pic**k**pock**e**t
Lösungsworte: keys, handbag

7 1. glove; 2. purse; 3. handbag; 4. rucksack; 5. skirt; 6. pipe; 7. beard; 8. gun; 9. shirt; 10. coat

8 1. fair; 2. good-looking; 3. normal; 4. lonely

9

d	**r**	**o**	**p**	**c**	a	z	j
b	m	**s**	**h**	**o**	**o**	**t**	k
r	u	**p**	r	**m**	f	s	**l**
o	**j**	**u**	**m**	**p**	**d**	**s**	**i**
b	s	**s**	a	**l**	**e**	**n**	**f**
a	f	**h**	k	**e**	**s**	**i**	**t**
y	w	t	j	**t**	**i**	**f**	a
a	**r**	**g**	**u**	**e**	**g**	**f**	i
a	**d**	**d**	x	f	**n**	h	v

hinzufügen: to add; sich streiten: to argue; fertigstellen: to complete; entwerfen: to design; fallen lassen: to drop; springen: to jump; hochheben: to lift; schieben: to push; ausrauben: to rob; schießen: to shoot; schnüffeln: to sniff

10 A famous man with lots of money **married** a woman and then somebody **murdered** him. Everybody thinks his wife **killed** him. She needs help. Who can **solve** the mystery? Sherlock Holmes. He **notices** everything. He asks the wife and the servants questions and they **describe** what they saw and what happened. He calls the police and they **arrest** a servant. How did he know who did it? “Elementary, my dear Watson,” he says.

11

1. Der Hund von Sir Elliots Kindern schnüffelte immer an ihren (= deren) Besuchern.
2. Sir Elliots Diener kümmerte sich um die Hunde von dessen Erben (= um die Hunde der Töchter von Sir Elliot).
3. Die Zimmer der Diener befinden sich auf dem Dachboden des Haupthauses.
4. Der Freund der Familie war Sherlock Holmes.
5. Der Nachbar der Elliots tötete den Hund ihrer Töchter.

12

John: **Did you have** a good time in London?
Karen: Yes, I **went** to Camden Market.
John: **Did you buy** lots of clothes?
Karen: Yes, **I did,** and in the afternoon I **met** lots of famous people.
John: Who **did you meet?**
Karen: I **met** the Queen and Paul McCartney.
John: Oh, what **did they say?**
Karen: Oh, they **didn't speak.** They **weren't** real. I **saw** them at Madame Tussauds, the famous wax museum.

13 Have you visited London before?
No, I haven't. I haven't been here before.
My brother has lived here for three years.
What has he done here?
He's learnt English and has met lots of nice people.

14 I've already seen three museums.
John visited Buckingham Palace yesterday.
Have you ever met the Queen?
What did you do last week?

15 *Mum:* **Have you done** anything exciting yet?
Sue: Yes, I **have.** I **have already been** on the London Eye. And yesterday I **went** to Camden Market.
Mum: Oh, I**'ve never been** there. **Was it** nice?
Sue: Yes, it **was.** I **bought** a leather handbag there. But somebody **has already stolen** it.
Mum: Oh no. When **did that happen?**
Sue: Last night when I **went** to the Notting Hill Carnival. But don't worry. The police **have just called.** They have already found it.

16 Notting Hill Carnival took place for the first time in 1964.
People have enjoyed it for 20 years.
Yesterday evening I danced in the streets.
I have never eaten such interesting food.

17 What **were you doing** at 12 o'clock last night?
I **was reading** a scary book.
My brothers **were looking** for monsters under the bed.
And **was your dad watching** TV?
No, **he wasn't.** My dad **was working.**
My older sister **was dancing** in a disco.
We **weren't sleeping** but we didn't hear the thieves.
They **were driving** our car away.

18 Was the boy buying something? – No, he wasn't. He was stealing something.
Was the girl listening to music? – Yes, she was.
Were they eating chips? – No, they weren't. They were eating ice-cream.
Were they visiting London? – No, they weren't. They were planning their trip.

19 What were you doing yesterday at 6 o'clock at the tube station? – I was waiting for a train. A man was stealing my purse. But the police were watching.

20 I was walking though London when I saw Buckingham Palace.
While I was taking a photo, the Queen arrived.
She was walking in the garden when she invited me for a cup of tea.
She showed me her house while we were waiting for the tea.
When I saw the swimming pool, William was swimming in it.
I fell asleep while I was sitting in a living room.
When I woke up, I was sitting at my desk at home.

21
1. He broke his leg while they were playing football./While they were playing football, he broke his leg.
2. A woman was riding a horse when her mobile rang./When her mobile rang, a woman was riding a horse.
3. While the man was listening to his radio, he fell asleep./The man fell asleep while he was listening to his radio.

22 I **was travelling** to Covent Garden on the Tube when I **met** a friend. While we **were talking,** the train **stopped** at Covent Garden. The doors **were closing** when my friend **said**, "Didn't you want to get off here?" I got off and the train **was leaving** when I **remembered** that my bag was still on the train. My mobile phone, my money and my train ticket were in the bag. I was just thinking, "What can I do now?" when I **saw** another friend. One phone call and ten minutes later I had my bag again.

23
1. I **visited** the Globe Theatre because I **had heard** that it was interesting.
2. We **bought** some tickets for a play after we **had visited** the theatre.
3. When we **saw** the play, I **had** already **read** the book by Shakespeare.
4. The play **had started** when we **arrived** at the theatre.
5. After I **had seen** the play, I **wanted** to become an actress.

24
1. The bus **had (already) left** when she **got to** the bus stop.
2. The play **had (already) started** before she **arrived** at the theatre.

25 I **had already eaten** breakfast when Mary called and suggested that we go on the London Eye that day. When I **arrived** at the London Eye, there was a big queue. That didn't matter because I **had already bought** tickets on the Internet. We **had agreed** to meet at 10 so I bought the tickets for 10.30. At 10.30 Mary had still not arrived so I **decided** to go on my own. I had already entered the capsule when I **saw** Mary. I jumped out again and ran to Mary. We **had just entered** a second capsule when the London Eye broke down. Lots of people were in the air and couldn't get down. "Oh, I am glad you were late," I said.

26 **D)** ist richtig.

27 1. Shirley drinks tea.
2. Grandma likes music and drinks milk.
3. Kevin goes to school.
4. The milkman likes music and knows Jean and Doris.
5. Jean drinks tea, drinks milk and lives near Grandma.
6. Doris drinks tea and lives near Grandma.

28 1. line 19: "Hm. So he knows where your purse is," ...
2. line 45: "I like that music," he said. "What is it? Is it Mozart?"
3. line 54: "He always listens to that Discman of his, doesn't he?"

29 1. Shirley wasn't sitting in the kitchen. She was sitting in the living room.
2. The milkman didn't put the milk in the fridge. He looked around the kitchen.
3. Grandma didn't look around the kitchen. She put the milk in the fridge.

30 1. She had a cup of tea. 2. Waits for his mum. 3. Shoes. 4. Beethoven. 5. Tea. 6. Shirley's purse.

31
Xx: market, normal
xX: parade, within
Xxx: colourful, skeleton
xXx: detective, cathedral

32
Mother: Where have you been? Why are you back so late from your day trip to London?
Calvin: Oh mum. I've had a terrible day. You won't believe it when I tell you what happened.
Mother: Why, what happened? Did you get lost?
Calvin: No, I didn't. I stayed with my class and we visited the Tower of London.
Mother: Oh, was it interesting?
Calvin: Yes, it was really interesting. We saw the Great Tower but the most interesting part was the dungeons. But we'd just got there when I needed to go to the toilet so I went to find one. When I got back to the dungeons, I couldn't find my class. They had already left. I looked in some more dungeons and then I found a door which looked interesting. I opened the door and went in. I hadn't found the light when the door closed behind me. I shouted, "Help. Let me out," but nobody opened the door. I was scared and I didn't know what to do. I shouted again and then I heard a noise. I waited for the door to open but it didn't open. Then I saw a light and a

head. It was a ghost's head. I wanted to run away but I couldn't move my legs because I was so scared. But then the ghost said, "Follow me. I'll show you how to get out." I followed her upstairs and downstairs and through some doors and then she pointed at a white door. "You can get out there," she said. I looked at the door and when I looked back she had gone. I went through the door and came out outside the White Tower. I didn't feel very good so I sat down and when I had had a drink and a sandwich, I felt better. I'd just stood up again when my teacher came round the corner. He was very angry. He thought that I'd sat there all the time and that I wasn't interested. It wasn't fair. I told him what had happened, but he didn't believe me.

Mother: Calvin. That was a great story but now tell me what really happened.

Calvin: Oh, Mum.

richtige Reihenfolge: 2 – 5 – 7 – 1 – 3 – 4 – 6 – 8

33 **part 1:**

Mary: So what should we do at the weekend?

Tom: Well, how about a trip to London? We could go to the Science Museum.

Mary: That's a good idea. I'd really like to go on the London Eye and I'd love to see the Tower of London.

Jean: Oh, but that's so expensive.

Mary: Yes, I know, but it's really interesting and you can spend all day in the Tower.

Jean: OK. Well, let's go to London then. But how should we get there?

Mary: We can go by train. Shall I get a timetable?

Tom: No, we can look on the Internet and we can buy the tickets right away, too.

Mary: OK. Let's do that. And why don't we check what's on at the theatre, too? Maybe we can get some tickets now.

Tom: Good idea. But shouldn't we ask our parents first?

Mary: Yes, that's a good idea. Maybe they'll give us some money.

part 2:

Mary: Excuse me. How much are the tickets, please?

Woman: Well, which play would you like to see?

Mary: We'd like to see Romeo and Juliet this afternoon, please.

Woman: Well, let me see. We've got some tickets at 33 pounds.

Mary: Oh, that's expensive. Are there special prices for children?

Woman: It's cheaper if you're under 16. But we also have tickets which cost five pounds if you want to stand.

Mary: Oh, that's a good idea. Yes, can I have three tickets, please? And where can I get a brochure, please?
Woman: You can get some in that shop over there. And that'll be 15 pounds for the tickets, please.
Mary: Here you are. Can we take photos in the theatre?
Woman: No, the actors don't like that but there are lots of good photos in the brochures there.
Mary: OK, thank you.

Excuse me. – part 2
Well, how about a trip to London? – part 1
And where can I get a brochure, please? – part 2
Can we take photos in the theatre? – part 2
How much are the tickets, please? – part 2
And why don't we check what's on at the theatre, too? – part 1
We could go to the Science Museum. – part 1
That's a good idea. – part 1
... how should we get there? – part 1
We'd like to see Romeo and Juliet this afternoon, please. – part 2
Shall I get a timetable? – part 1
Are there special prices for children? – part 2

34 They want to go to London by **train.**
They want to buy some tickets for the **train** on the Internet.
They buy **three** tickets which cost **five** pounds at the theatre.
They **mustn't** take photos in the theatre.

Skills workshop 2

1
1. Datteln
2. Datum
3. mit (jdm.) gehen
4. umziehen
5. sich (weg-)bewegen
6. sich umziehen
7. Wechselgeld

2 1. b); 2. c); 3. c); 4. a)

3
1. Everybody can be a detective.
2. The servant was the murderer.

4 1. im siebten Himmel; 2. vollkommen unverständlich („Das sind böhmische Dörfer für mich.“)

Revision A (Unit 1–2)

1 1. goal**k**eeper; 2. beard; 3. um**p**ire; 4. goggl**e**s; 5. ne**p**hew; 6. s**k**ateboarder; 7. assi**st**ant; 8. boot; 9. gl**o**ve; 10. de**te**ctive; 11. **c**hef; 12. ra**ck**et
keyword: pickpocket

2 to smoke a pipe; to notice a clue; to design a building; to solve a mystery; to marry a woman; to shoot a gun; to change one's mind; to score a goal

3

infinitive	*simple past*	*past participle*	*German*
to begin	began	begun	anfangen
to become	became	become	werden
to break	broke	broken	(zer-)brechen
to catch	caught	caught	fangen
to feel	felt	felt	fühlen
to hit	hit	hit	schlagen
to shake	shook	shook	zittern
to shoot	shot	shot	schießen

4
1. When I **saw** the poster, I **had (already/just) learnt** some new tricks.
2. The competition **had (just/already) started** when I **arrived.**
3. I **had practised** for two minutes when I **broke** my skateboard.
4. After I**'d borrowed** a skateboard, I **won** the competition.

5 What do you usually do on Saturdays? – I usually play tennis with my dad. – What are you doing tomorrow? – We aren't playing tennis. We are watching a match at Wimbledon. My dad knows an umpire there. He is talking to his friend now. – Who is playing tomorrow? – My favourite star is going to play in the final.

6 I was running along the street when I saw the bus.
I was sitting on the bus when the bus broke down.

7 My dreams **have come true;** I've met a girl who likes me, too. I saw her first while a boy **was robbing** her in London. She **was waiting** at a bus stop when he **pushed** her and she dropped her rucksack. I **had just got off** a bus and I helped her to pick her things up and call the police. She thanked me and we **chatted** to each other for an hour. We didn't even notice that it **had started** to rain.

How can I describe her? Well, she's funny she's good at sport. When we **play** tennis, she can hit the ball hard. She **makes** me laugh and I always **feel** happy when she's there. **I'm meeting** her tomorrow. We**'re going** to London again. And will we marry? I don't know. But if things go wrong, it **doesn't matter,** she's got a really nice friend, too.

8

Mutter: Frag sie bitte, was wir nicht verpassen sollten.
Du: **What shouldn't we miss in London?**
Wirtin: Well, why don't you go on the London Eye? The view is great.
Du: **Sie schlägt vor, dass wir zum London Eye gehen. Die Aussicht sei super.**
Vater: Das ist eine gute Idee. Wie kommen wir dahin?
Du: **That's a good idea. How do we get there?**
Wirtin: Well, you can take the Central Line to Bank. That's westbound. Then change at Bank to the Northern Line. Get off at London Bridge. That's the first stop and you can walk from there.
Du: **Wir können die Central Line in Richtung Westen Richtung nehmen. Dann steigen wir bei Bank um und fahren mit der Northern Line eine Haltestelle bis zur London Bridge. Von dort können wir laufen.**
Mutter: Danke sehr! Frag sie noch, ob der Buckingham Palace auch in der Nähe ist.
Du: **Thank you very much. And is Buckingham Palace far from there?**
Wirtin: It isn't very far. You can walk there or you can take the Jubilee Line northbound to Green Park. That's only two stops.
Du: **Es ist nicht sehr weit. Wir können laufen oder die Jubilee Line nehmen, Richtung Norden bis Green Park. Das sind nur zwei Haltestellen.**
Vater: Thanks very much.

9

Susan: So how was the game? Did you win?
Mike: I don't know.
Susan: What do you mean you don't know?
Mike: Well, they were still arguing about it when I had to leave. It was the strangest game I've ever played.
Susan: Why? What happened?
Mike: Well, not much in the first half. We played better but we just couldn't get a goal.
Susan: Well, what's new there?
Mike: Ha ha. Anyway. We'd just come back on the pitch again after the break when one of their players got the ball and ran the wrong way with it.
Susan: The wrong way?
Mike: Yeah, the wrong way! He just didn't notice. He'd kicked the ball at

the goal when he noticed his goalkeeper was standing in it. Anyway the goalkeeper couldn't stop it.

Susan: So that was one – nil to you.

Mike: Yep. But we were still laughing when they scored another goal – for them this time.

Susan: So that was one – one.

Mike: Yep. And the game was really exciting from then on. But there were no more goals until we scored another one after we'd played for about ninety minutes.

Susan: So that was 2 – 1. You won.

Mike: Yes – and no.

Susan: What?

Mike: Well, the referee's clock had stopped. And the game was so exciting that nobody even looked at the time for another ten minutes.

Susan: So what difference does it make?

Mike: Well, we don't know if we scored before the end of the game or not.

Susan: But if the referee hadn't stopped the game then you scored before the end, didn't you? That's it. Two – one.

Mike: That's what we said but the other team said it's not fair and we should have another match.

Susan: And? What do you think?

Mike: Oh, I think we should play again. I just love football.

richtige Reihenfolge: 4 – 2 – 1 – 3 – 5

10 Venus and Serena Williams are sisters. Their father taught them to play tennis. Their father had learnt about tennis from a video. The Williams' family grew up in Los Angeles and they didn't have much money. Their father wanted them to do well at sport so that they could have a better life. They worked hard and they had already won lots of matches before they were even 14 years old.

Unit 3

1 Have you got something to say? Well, we've got people who want to listen. You think you aren't a **poet?** Are you sure? Have you tried to write a poem? No? Well, try now. Have you had an **argument** with your **girlfriend** and you're sad? Well, write it down and let it out. Then practise! At our poetry slams the **performance** is almost as important as the poem itself. But don't worry you'll get a bad **response** – we show **respect** to all our slamsters. Winners can win a prize, but this isn't about prizes. It's about **poetry.**

2 1. **prim**ary **s**ch**o**ol; 2. gramma**r** sc**h**ool; 3. Adva**n**ced Le**ve**ls; 4. **college**
Lösungswort: comprehensive

3 1. eyebrow; 2. tongue; 3. cottage; 4. mirror; 5. leaf; 6. wave

4 sad – happy; stupid – clever; alive – dead; weak – strong; calm – nervous;
übrig bleibt: frustrated – frustriert

5 I sometimes think I should **make/take** notes before I talk to my parents so that I don't say the wrong thing. I often **have** an argument with them if I want to do something that they are not happy with. My mum **gets** into such a state when she sees my tattoo and my dad **has** a fit when he sees my pierced nose. Maybe I shouldn't talk to them at all, I should just **leave** messages on the answering machine.

6

p	**i**	**e**	**r**	**c**	**e**	f	h	p	l
d	**n**	t	r	**l**	x	e	**b**	**e**	**t**
f	**v**	i	a	**i**	m	b	y	s	a
q	**e**	z	u	**c**	**a**	**r**	**e**	g	**c**
j	**n**	**m**	w	**k**	m	i	v	b	**o**
l	**t**	**o**	s	j	u	k	c	r	**n**
t	t	**v**	s	g	m	n	j	z	**t**
o	**p**	**e**	**r**	**f**	**o**	**r**	**m**	e	**a**
y	i	c	o	p	r	z	f	b	**c**
c	**h**	**o**	**k**	**e**	f	**t**	**e**	**x**	**t**

erfinden: invent;
druchstechen: pierce;
klicken: click; aufführen: perform;
umziehen: move; wetten: bet;
sich kümmern: care;
sich in Verbindung setzen: contact;
keine Luft bekommen: choke;
eine SMS schicken: text

7 What a disaster!
It's just not fair.
It's driving me crazy!
Oh, that's terrible.
We must do something!

8
1. I'm just calling to say I'll be home late.
2. Could you call me back, please?
3. Can I take a message?
4. Can you spell it for me, please?
5. Sorry, I can't take your call now.
6. I'd like to speak to Chris.

9 Es eignen sich die Sätze **1 und 2.**

10
1. – Gemma was nervous, wasn't she? She told **me** before the slam.
   + But **her** poem was very good, wasn't it?
   – Yes, **it** was. It was much better than **mine.** My poem wasn't very good. Has **she** written many poems?
   + Yes, **she** has. The poem in our school newspaper is **hers.**
2. – What do the winners win?
   + **They** win a place on a course. Famous poets give **them** lessons and somebody prints **their** poems.
3. – Well done! **You**'ve won. **Your** poem was great.
   + Thanks, but the poem wasn't **mine.**
   – What do you mean it wasn't **yours?**
   + John wrote it. It was **his.** But **he** was too nervous to perform.

11
1. I'll visit you.
2. I'll look.
3. I'll help you pack.
4. I'll carry them.
5. I'll phone (you) every day.

12 1.
Boy: I've got two tickets for the baseball match but I don't know anybody who wants to come with me.
Boy: Oh, I'll come with you.
2.
Girl: Oh, I'm really nervous about the tennis match. I'm playing really badly at the moment.
Girl: Oh, I'm sure you'll win.

3.
Girl: Let's meet on Saturday morning.
Boy: No, I play football with my friends then.
4.
Girl: Hey, you're great at skateboarding.
Boy: Thanks.
Girl: And that trick looks really good. Will you teach it to me?
Boy: Yes, OK.
5.
Boy: Oh no. My skis are broken.
Woman: Don't worry. I'll buy you some new ones.
6.
Girl: Which sports do you usually do?
Boy: I run in the 100 metres.
7.
Girl: You can't enter the competition. You have to be over 12.
Boy: I'll be 13 next Friday.

1. Oh, I'**ll come** with you. (spontane Reaktion)
2. Oh, I'm sure, you'**ll** win.
3. No, I **play** football with my friends then.
4. **Will you teach** it to me? (spontane Reaktion)
5. I'**ll buy** you some new ones. (spontane Reaktion)
6. I **run** in the 100 metres.
7. I'**ll be** 13 next Friday.

13
Wendy: Look! Yvonne is tired now. Liz **is going to win** the match.
Chris: I don't know. Look at those clouds. We'**re going to have** a storm soon and then they'**ll stop** the match.
Wendy: I hope they **won't stop** the match.
Chris: Did you phone Tim? **Are you going to meet/Are you meeting** him later?
Wendy: Yes, I called him. He'**s going to come/'s coming** here at three and we'**re going to play/'re playing** tennis. Do you want to play, too?
Chris: Oh, I think I'**ll go** home. I don't want to get wet.

14 I've just moved to a **beautiful** place in Wales but I don't know if I like it here yet. I've met some **nice** kids at school but I miss my **old** friends **terribly.** I've found a **good** rap club so I can go there in the evening. Some of the kids play really **well** and I want to learn, too. Maybe if I try **hard,** I'll be **happy** soon.

15 Liz's poem was **the best** and Paul's poem was **the worst.** Susan performed **more beautifully** than Paul but Liz performed **the most beautifully.** The audience's response to Susan's poem was **better** than to Paul's. After they had heard Liz's poem, the audience response was **the most excited.**

16 John had an **exciting** girlfriend but she left him because he was too **boring** for her. John was **sadder** than ever before. He worked **harder** than he had planned and wrote a poem. Was it **better** than other poems? He didn't know but it said what he wanted to say.
He was sitting **quietly** at a poetry slam when he decided to let it out. He thought he must be the **most stupid** person in the room but he performed **(the most) brilliantly.** Not a person in the room thought he was boring.

17 If it rains on Saturday afternoon, Jane **will go** to the cinema. She wants to go with Ben, Joe, Rosy and Carol, but if Ben **goes,** Joe won't go – he doesn't like Ben. Jane loves funny films and scary films. If they **go** to see a scary film, Rosy and Ben **won't go** and if they **don't go** to see a scary film, Carol **won't go.** Who **will go** with her if they go to see a funny film?
→ Jane will go with **Rosy and Ben.**

18 If my sister's boyfriend asks her, she'll marry him.
My dad won't be happy if she marries him soon.
If they marry, my sister will leave home.
If my sister leaves home, I'll have my own room. Hurray.
Will I be happy if I have my own room?

19 What will you do at the weekend if it rains?
I'll do my homework while it rains/it's raining.
As soon as it stops, I'll go outside.
When it goes dark, I'll go home again.

20 I've just hurt **myself.**
Bye everybody! I hope you all enjoyed **yourselves.**
She often talks to **herself.**
They made that CD **themselves.**
Jane! Don't drive **yourself** crazy with that homework. Let me help.

21 It was Friday. I got up and then got dressed ~~myself~~ as always. I was late and had to hurry ~~myself~~, as always. I went to school, worked hard and behaved myself – as always! I got home, sat down ~~myself~~ and relaxed ~~myself~~ – as always. My dad made dinner and hurt himself with a knife – as always. I ate dinner and got ready ~~myself~~ for youth club – as always – on a Friday! When I got to youth club, I met ~~myself~~ a girl. We laughed and enjoyed ourselves. I felt ~~myself~~ happy – as always. But nothing now was as always – everything had changed ~~itself~~.

22 Did you really make it yourselves?
John wrote it himself.
I don't want to ask him myself.
You have to find it yourself.
Can we cook dinner ourselves?

23
1. Hey. Stop it! You're going to hurt yourself.
2. Well, thank you for coming. Have you enjoyed yourselves?
3. Isn't that picture good? Do you think he drew it himself?
4. She's really good at music. She taught herself to play the piano, you know?
5. No, we want to do it ourselves.
6. They tidied their room themselves.

1. yourself → reflexiv
2. yourselves → reflexiv
3. himself → verstärkend
4. herself → reflexiv
5. ourselves → verstärkend
6. themselves → verstärkend

24 We wrote the play ourselves.
Everybody got ready.
We had to hurry (up).
I was the star and I couldn't relax.
But everybody enjoyed themselves.

25
1. They met **each other.**
2. They looked at **themselves.**
3. They looked at **each other.**
4. They taught **themselves** to build a boat.
5. They took photos of **each other.**

26 Tuesday – Wednesday – Saturday

27 1. b); 2. c); 3. a); 4. a); 5. c); 6. b)

28 1. true; 2. not in the text; 3. true; 4. false

29 My mum and dad had a big argument (lines 6/7).
There's a youth club here so if it's easy to find, I'll go on Friday (line 22).
I'm sure you can imagine how nervous I was (lines 45/46).

30 1. hat; 2. bark; 3. ship; 4. cheap; 5. bring; 6. life; 7. bed; 8. sad; 9. harm; 10. fit; 11. bet; 12. bought

31
Mum: Can we talk about last night?
Nic: Yeah. If we have to.
Mum: You were very late home. If you don't get home early enough, you'll have to stay at home in ...
Nic: But it wasn't late! And that's not fair. I'm fourteen, Mum. All my friends can stay out until 12 o'clock and I have to be home at 10 on a Saturday. That's not fair.
Mum: I'm not interested in what your friends' parents think. I am your mum and you need enough sleep.
Nic: But I can sleep late on Sunday and still have enough sleep.
Mum: Well, that's true, but I worried about you last night. I didn't know where you were. And that's not fair.
Nic: Can we talk about it in the future? Will you listen to my opinion, too? If we agree on a time together, I won't be late again.
Mum: OK, fine. I'll let you stay out later on Saturday if do all your homework first.
Nic: OK, great. Er. And Mum ...
Mum: Yes.
Nic: Can I go out tonight?

1. Can we talk about last night?
2. If you don't get home early (enough), you'll have to stay at home in ...
3. I'm not interested in what your friends' parents think.
4. Well, that's true, but I worried about you last night.
5. If we agree on a time together, I won't be late again.
6. I'll let you stay out later on Saturday if do all your homework first.

1. Mum; 2. Mum; 3. Mum; 4. Mum; 5. Nic; 6. Mum

32 **Phone call 1:**

Ann's Mum: This is 736 8243. Hello.
Kylie: Hi. Here's Kylie. Is Ann there?
Ann's Mum: No, she isn't here. She isn't back from tennis club yet.
Kylie: Oh, could you ask her to call me back, please?
Ann's Mum: Yes, of course. She should be back in a minute. Should she call you at home or your mobile?
Kylie: Oh, at home. I'm trying to do my Maths homework and I just can't do it.
Ann's Mum: Oh OK. Well, I don't think she's done her homework yet but I'll tell her.

a) to Ann, b) at the tennis club, c) call her back

Phone call 2:

Answering machine: Sorry, we can't answer the phone at the moment. If you'd like to leave a message after the tone, we'll call you back.
Diana: Hi. This is Diana. I'm just calling to say I can't go to the cinema this evening. I'm going to be home late. Maybe we can go tomorrow. Can you call me back tomorrow morning, please? Thanks. See you.

a) Diana, b) She can't go to the cinema tonight. c) tomorrow morning

Phone call 3:

Neil: Hello.
Man: Hello. This is Tariq Kumar. I'd like to speak to your dad, please.
Neil: Oh, I'm afraid he isn't in at the moment. Can I take a message?
Man: Yes, please. Could you tell him that I called and could he call me back, please?
Neil: Yes. Just a moment. I'm sorry, I didn't understand your name. Could you spell it for me, please?
Man: Yes, of course. It's Tariq Kumar. That's T – A – R – I – Q Kumar, K – U – M – A – R.
Neil: OK, I've got that. Does my dad have your phone number?
Man: Yes, I think so but I'll give it to you again. It's 0162 245 7634.
Neil: Er. 0162 245 7634.
Man: Yes, that's right. Thanks a lot.
Neil: You're welcome. Goodbye.

a) Tariq Kumar, b) 0162 245 7634, c) call him back

Skills workshop 3

1

Scene 1

Chris: Hey, what do you think about these?
Sue: Well, they're nice, but I always wear trousers. I'd really like to buy a new skirt for my birthday party. A short one.
Chris: If you buy a very short one, your mum will never let you wear it.
Sue: Yeah, I know. Well, it doesn't have to be that short.
Chris: What about this dress? You'd look good in this.
Sue: Yeah, that's really cool, and I'd get it if I had more money. But have you seen the price?
Chris: Oh yeah.
Sue: I'd like to try these skirts on but where's the assistant?
Chris: Er. Hey, isn't that your boyfriend over there?
Sue: Where? Where? Oh, yeah. Oh, and look. He's with Jane.
Chris: Oh yeah. I didn't see her.
Sue: What are they doing together?
Chris: Er ...
Sue: Look at them. They're having a great time together. Look! He's got his arm on her shoulders. Oh no!
Chris: Hey Sue. Sue, come back. Oh no.

Scene 2

Mum: Sue, do you want something to eat?
Sue: No, I'm not hungry.
Mum: Oh Sue. You must eat something. You haven't eaten all day. Oh, there's the phone again. Sue, you answer it. It's probably Jane again. She's already tried to phone you three times.
Sue: I don't want to talk to her.
Mum: Why not? What's happened? She's one of your best friends.
Sue: No, she isn't. If she was my friend, she wouldn't go out with my boyfriend.
Mum: What do you mean?
Sue: I saw her yesterday in town. And she was with Steve. They were both laughing and really enjoying themselves. They weren't thinking about me. That was clear.
Mum: Maybe it wasn't how you thought. If you spoke to her, you'd find out.

Scene 3

Mum: Hi Jane. Come in. She's just in there.
Jane: Hi Sue. Happy Birthday.
Sue: I don't want to talk to you.
Jane: Oh Sue. Chris has told me why you're angry. You saw me and Steve together in town, didn't you?
Sue: Yes. Oh Jane. How could you do it? I thought you were my friend.
Jane: Yes, I am. And if you thought well of me, you would know that I would never go out with your boyfriend.
Sue: I never thought you would. But you have to believe your eyes, don't you?
Jane: Yes, but what did you see? You saw me and Steve in your favourite shop, didn't you? Do you think I'm so stupid? If I wanted to go out with your boyfriend, I wouldn't go to your favourite shop. Would I? Use your head. What do you think we were doing in your favourite shop just before your birthday?
Sue: Er ... you weren't ... er ...
Jane: Yes, I was. I was helping Steve to find a present for you.
Sue: Oh no. Have you told Steve?
Jane: No, if you want to tell him about your mistake, you'll have to tell him yourself.

Scene 1: c); Scene 2: a); Scene 3: b)

2 1. b); 2. a); 3. c); 4. b); 5. c)

3 1. Chris; 2. Sue; 3. Sue's Mum; 4. Sue; 5. Jane

Test practice B

1 1. true; 2. true; 3. false; 4. true; 5. not in the text; 6. false; 7. false

2 3. Oliver wants to go shopping alone/without his dad.
6. Children in India, Pakistan and other countries make the trainers.
7. Oliver watched a DVD about child labour at home.

3 1. Well, buy them yourself then. (l. 12)
2. For indoors or outdoors? (l. 16)
3. They're half the price. (l. 28)
4. You're joking. (l. 34)
5. Oliver's dad can't believe his ears. (l. 30)
6. I feel sorry for all the children. (l. 38)
7. It won't make any difference to them. (l. 40)

4 Da steht, dass diese Turnschuhe gut für die Füße sind. Sie eignen sich sehr gut für Hallensportarten, zum Beispiel Badminton, Tischtennis und Tennis. Und sie wurden ohne Kinderarbeit hergestellt.

5 Oliver, his sister Mary and their parents have just watched the programme about child labour.

Mary: Well, I still don't understand why you didn't want to buy the trainers or why you won't wear them. If we don't buy the shoes, the children won't have any work and they won't have any money. They won't have enough to eat. That's terrible.

Oliver: If nobody buys the shoes, then they'll have to give the jobs to the adults. They'll have to pay them more. They'll have more money in the end. And it'll cost us more but that's OK because ...

Mary: But some of those children's parents were ill or one of their parents had died. What about those children? Isn't it better that they can work and live?

Oliver: No! Yes! Oh, of course it's better that they can live ... but they shouldn't have to work. People should look after the children. Oh, I don't know if we can solve all the problems in the world but we can try to do something, can't we?

Mary: Yes, we can. Maybe we should tell other people, too. Then other people won't buy the shoes or other clothes and things they can make.

Oliver: Yes, that's a good idea. We could make a poster and put it up at school.
Mary: Yes, let's do it.

1. a); 2. a), b) und c)

6 **Help change children's lives!**
Some firms use child labour in their factories. We think this is wrong. The children should not have to work. They should go to school.
If we don't buy the shoes, the factories will give the jobs to their parents.
We have written a list below of firms which use child labour. Think about it when you are buying clothes. The cheapest clothes aren't always the best.
Choose carefully!

Unit 4

1 The northwest of England is famous for its **industry** – the Industrial Revolution started here and one reason for this was all the coal in the area. Most of the **coal mines** are now closed but there are still many **factories** here. But it is also a beautiful **region.** Away from the cities the **landscape** is wild with many **mountains** and lakes. The **coastline** is lovely, too, and there are some great beaches along it. And you should not miss Liverpool's **waterfront.**

2 The Welsh **coast** is beautiful with many cliffs and beaches.
There were once many **smugglers** along the coast.
It does rain a lot so you often see clouds in the **sky**.
There is a strong **tradition** of music in Wales.
In fact many famous **singers** and actors come from Wales.

3 1. suitcase; 2. luggage; 3. trolley; 4. cliff; 5. stone; 6. ferry; 7. mountain; 8. dragon

4 ¼: a/one quarter; ½: a/one half; ¾: three quarters; 1 ½: one and a half

5 a **valuable** painting; a **helpless** baby; an **independent** woman; an **ancient** building

6 1. to smell; 2. to sound; 3. to look; 4. to feel; 5. to taste; 6. to hear; 7. to look; 8. to seem; 9. to touch

7

s	a	**c**	**l**	**i**	**m**	**b**	d
d	**e**	**f**	**i**	**n**	**e**	**o**	g
a	w	z	j	h	i	**t**	r
m	l	**t**	**u**	**g**	y	**h**	e
a	b	**r**	s	e	q	**e**	k
g	a	**u**	r	h	b	**r**	u
e	l	**s**	**c**	**a**	**t**	**c**	**h**
q	a	**t**	m	s	z	d	n
n	j	u	z	**r**	x	s	e
p	**r**	**o**	**t**	**e**	**c**	**t**	a
m	d	n	r	**s**	g	m	i
r	h	e	i	**t**	k	a	l

festnehmen: to catch;
klettern: to climb;
sich ausruhen: to rest;
schützen: to protect;
definieren: to define;
stören; to bother;
vertrauen: to trust;
zupfen: to tug;
beschädigen: to damage

8 My mum had to go **away** for a few days so we had to look **after** ourselves and the house. My mum usually organises everything so everything went wrong while she was away. We got **up** late every day and were always late for school. We never put our shoes **away** when we took them **off** so we couldn't find them again later. One day we looked **for** my sister's shoes for 20 minutes. When she got **to** school, she saw that she had put **on** two different ones. My dad's a terrible cook and had to look **up** the recipes for anything he cooked. One day while he was cooking spaghetti bolognaise, all the lights went **out.** We got takeaways after that. My mum came back on the Friday. She came in the door, looked **at** the kitchen and walked out again. "Call me again when it's clean," she said, "I'll be **at** your grandma's house."

9

1. One cat is **in front of** the house and another one is **behind** it.
2. She went **into** the house and then walked **out of** it again.
3. House A is **opposite** house B.

10

I'd like to know if there are any good museums here.
Yes, there's a really interesting one in the city centre.
I need to find a hotel which isn't too expensive.
Why don't you try the Midland? That doesn't cost too much.
Do you have any information about smugglers in the area?
Yes, we do. Would you like some leaflets?

11 Could you tell me the time of the next train to Swansea, please?
What platform does it leave from? (*auch möglich, aber unüblich:* From what platform does it leave?)
Do I have to change trains?
Is there a bus to the airport?

12
1. Shirley Bassey is a famous Welsh singer whose father came from Nigeria.
2. Wales is a country whose road signs are usually in two languages.
3. Most people whose first language is Welsh speak English, too.

13
1. Hey. Is that the boy whose brother is in our class?
2. Do you know anybody who's really good at rugby?
3. There are some rugby clubs whose players do a lot of work with children.
4. We have a neighbour who's a famous Welsh singer.

1. whose; 2. who's; 3. whose; 4. who's

14
1. How much are the apples? – The green **ones** or the red **ones?**
2. I'd like to look at that bag. – Which **one?** The big, brown **one?**
3. How much are those sandwiches? – These cheese **ones** are £1.50.

15
1. The big ones are/cost 30 pence.
2. The one on the wall?
3. Which one? This one?
4. This yellow one?
5. Do you mean those ones over there?

16 People **who** become very good at sport have to train very hard for many years. It helps if they have a sports club **which** is good in their area. And it's always easier for children **whose** friends like sport, too. There are also people **who** have bodies **which** are better for one sport or another. For example, people **whose** legs are longer are often better at running. And, of course, for some sports it's easier for children **whose** parents can buy them good equipment or lessons.

17 I met some people who were very nice.
I heard some music which was great.
I stayed with people whose mother sang in a famous choir.
I visited some beaches which were beautiful.
The people who owned the hotel spoke English and Welsh.

18 Golf is a sport which is very popular in England but it is not a sport ~~that~~ most people think is very exciting. In fact there are people who think that golf isn't a sport at all because they think of old people who walk slowly around a big field or two and every ten minutes or so hit a ball. I was once one of those people. I'm a person who loves most sport but I thought that golf was very boring. How wrong I was! A friend ~~who~~ I've known for years and loves golf bought me a lesson for my birthday. It was a present ~~which~~ I didn't really want but you can't say no, can you? And I'm glad I didn't say, "No, thank you," because it was one of the best presents ~~that~~ I've ever had. I loved the lesson and I've loved golf ever since. It's great fun when you play with people ~~who~~ you like and it makes you healthy. You often walk ten kilometres in places which are very tiring while you are carrying a bag which is very heavy.

19 Die beste Zusammenfassung ist **C).**

20 1. b); 2. b); 3. b); 4. c); 5. c)

21 1. boat; 2. bed; 3. hole

22 They waited and waited in the boat. More water came in and they became colder and colder. Every second seemed like an hour. Then the wind grew less strong. Just a little but they started to hope again. Then the boat hit the cliffs. The boat broke into small pieces and everybody jumped in the water. The water was cold, but the waves were smaller now and the lifeboat came nearer. It saved everybody.

23 stone – singer – smuggler – side – landscape – circle – suitcase

24 **Dialogue 1:**

Girl: Excuse me. It's cold in here. Could you close the window please?
Boy: But I think it's warm in here. Can't you put a pullover on?
Girl: Oh, I'll go and sit in another seat.
Boy: Oh, OK. Bye.

Dialogue 2:

Boy: Sorry to bother you, but could I sit there?
Woman: Yes, of course. Sorry. I'll just move my bag.
Boy: Thanks a lot.
Woman: Oh, that's no problem.

Dialogue 3:

Girl: Do you have any information about the museums here?
Woman: Yes, of course. Would you like some leaflets?
Girl: Yes, please. And are they easy to find?
Woman: Yes, they are all in the city centre. Here's a map for you.
Girl: Thanks a lot. Goodbye.
Woman: Goodbye.

1. dialogue 3; 2. dialogue 1; 3. dialogue 3; 4. dialogue 2; 5. dialogue 1; 6. dialogue 2

25
1. No, he doesn't.
2. She moves her bag.
3. Information about museums.
4. Leaflets and a map.

26
Luke: Hello.
Jill: Hi. It's me.
Luke: Hi Jill.
Jill: So what was it like?
Luke: It was OK. Brighton's nice. The house was OK. The country around Brighton is beautiful. We're going to live near the sea ...
Jill: You'll be able to go swimming before breakfast every day then.
Luke: Yeah, yeah. The school sounds good and I met a few kids who will be in my class. They seemed nice, too.
Jill: Great. You'll love it then.
Luke: I'm sure I will like it. I think Brighton's a really exciting place but I'll miss you, you know?
Jill: Ah, you'll forget me before Christmas.
Luke: I won't. I'll never forget you. Will you come and visit me?
Jill: If you ask me and my Mum says I can go. What can you do in Bristol then?
Luke: Well, the beach is great and they have lots of bands there in summer.
Jill: Oh, that sounds good. When are you moving?
Luke: We're moving at the end of July.
Jill: At the end of July? I thought you wanted to move at the end of August. And I thought you wanted to spend the summer with me.
Luke: Well, I do. You know that. But Mum and Dad want to move sooner so that they can sort everything out before they start work.
Jill: They probably want to enjoy the beach in summer, too.
Luke: Yes, well, why don't you come down and stay in the summer?
Jill: Oh, yes please. I could come down in August for your birthday.
Luke: Er, well, not for my birthday. I'm meeting some of the kids from my new school who I met when I went down.

Jill: Oh. Well, that's nice.
Luke: Yes, well, they asked me to a party. And Lisa's parents have got a swimming pool in the garden.
Jill: Lisa? Who's Lisa?
Luke: She's just a girl in my class. There'll be lots of boys there, too.
Jill: Yes, I am sure there will be. Well, have a good time, Luke.

Lösung: b)

27 1. a); 2. c); 3. b); 4. c); 5. b)

Skills workshop 4

1 William: the Isle of Wight or the Lake District (A or C)
Ellen: Newcastle or Bristol (B or D)
Maria: the Isle of Wight or the Lake District (A or C)
Liam: Newcastle or Bristol (B or D)

2 William: the Lake District (C)
Ellen: Bristol (B)
Maria: Isle of Wight (A)
Liam: Newcastle (D)

3
1. off the south coast of England
2. not very much
3. surfing, windsurfing
4. north of England, near the coast
5. its nightlife
6. football
7. in the northwest of England
8. walk, climb, canoe, sail, swim, dive, enjoy the views
9. wet/it rains a lot
10. Bath, South Wales, Cornwall, Devon, Dorset
11. its music and film industries
12. America

4 1. true; 2. not in the text; 3. false; 4. true; 5. false; 6. not in the text; 7. false;
Korrektur: 3. Not many tourists go to Newcastle. 5. You don't have to be very fit to walk in the Lake Distict. 7. Bristol has an airport.

Revision B (Unit 3–4)

1

1. trolley *(die anderen sind Gepäck[-stücke])*
2. poet *(die anderen können nur männlich sein)*
3. monastery *(die anderen sind Teile eines Hauses)*
4. aftershave *(die anderen sind Körperteile)*
5. channel *(die anderen haben keine zweite Bedeutung)*
6. choir *(die anderen sind Einzelpersonen)*

2

1. At a poetry slam the judges **hold up** a piece of paper with the number of points on it.
2. Where do you **hang out** on a Friday? – Oh, at the youth club.
3. Can you **take off** your shoes and then **put away** in the cupboard, please?
4. When the lights **go out** at the cinema, the film starts.

3

1. The mountains are very old. They're **ancient.**
2. She can look after herself. She's very **independent.**
3. You can think better if you stay **calm.**
4. He's **helpless.** He can't do anything himself.
5. She was the best but she didn't win. That's **unfair.**
6. He's very **frustrated.** He's tried again and again but he still can't do it.
7. She isn't strong. She's very **weak.**
8. If it's not dangerous, it's **safe.**

4

1. The person **who** lives in a house isn't always the **owner.**
2. The **tongue** is something **which** you talk with.
3. **Smugglers** are people **who** take things they shouldn't into countries.
4. A **cottage** is a small building **which** you can live in.
5. A **prince** is a person **whose** father is usually the king.
6. A **mirror** is something **which** you can see yourself in.

5

1. We had to carry almost everything ourselves.
2. I hurt myself as/when I sat down on a broken chair.
3. I can't meet my old friends now but we write to each other.
4. I can look after myself but I feel sad.

6 We're going to stay in the most beautiful cottage you have ever seen.
We're going to stay in a village which is near the sea.
There are many mountains there and I want to climb the highest one.
We're going to meet a friend of mine whose parents are Welsh.
I'll try to learn Welsh if they have time to help me.
I think Welsh people speak English more beautifully than English people.
We want to borrow a boat which we can sail ourselves.
If the weather is warm, we'll go swimming a lot.

7
1. I like that painting. – Which **one?**
2. Those shoes are nice. – Do you mean the green **ones?**
3. Let's buy some biscuits. – Yes, some chocolate **ones.**
4. How much is that cake, please? – That **one?**

8 Last summer I stayed on a farm, ~~a beautiful~~ → **a beautiful one** which had animals, and it was great. Life is very ~~differently~~ → **different** on a farm and I felt strange at first. The parents worked ~~hardly~~ → **hard** every day and they didn't have much time to relax ~~themselves~~, but life was ~~well~~ → **good**. They did almost everything ~~theyselves~~ → **themselves.** The mother made the bread, cheese and butter herself and it was the ~~good~~ → **best** food which I'd ever tasted. The children ~~who~~ → **whose** school was miles away were the fittest children ~~which~~ → **who/–** I have ever met. They are my friends now and ~~they~~ → **they'll** visit us in the school holidays if their parents agree. I enjoyed ~~me~~ → **myself** so much on the farm that I want to be a farmer now. It may be difficult but I'll learn even if I ~~will~~ have to ~~teach~~ → **teach myself** everything.

9
Ellis: Hello. This is 432 6887.
Woman: Hello, this is Cynthia Wallis here. Can I speak to your mother, please?
Ellis: I'm sorry, she isn't in at the moment. Can I take a message?
Woman: Yes, please. I can't meet her for tennis this evening. Can you ask her to call me back, please?
Ellis: Yes, does she have your number?
Woman: Yes, but wait a minute. When will she be home do you think?
Ellis: Well, at about four o'clock.
Woman: OK. Good. Can you give her my mobile number then, please? It's oh one seven three, four seven two, three double five one.
Ellis: Oh, one, seven, three, four, seven, two, three, double five, one. And I'm sorry, I didn't quite understand your name, please.
Woman: It's Cynthia. C – y – n – t – h – i – a. She'll know who I am.

Cynthia Wallis phoned. Her mobile number is 0173 472 3551. She can't play tennis this evening.

10 *Father:* Ich würde gern wissen, ob es dieses Wochenende Chorkonzerte gibt.
You: **We'd like to know if there are any choir concerts this weekend.**
Assistant: Let me see. Oh yes, there's a concert in Caerphilly this evening.
You: **Ja, es gibt heute Abend ein Konzert in Caerphilly.**
Father: Gibt es dazu Informationen?
You: **Do you have any information about it?**
Assistant: Yes, would you like some leaflets?
You: **Ja, möchtest du ein paar Flyer?**
Father: Ja bitte. Und wie kommt man nach Caerphilly?
You: **Yes please. And how can we get there?**
Assistant: You can get there by train.
You: **Wir können mit dem Zug hinfahren.**

11 1. false; 2. true; 3. true; 4. not in the text

12 Hi Jake,
I'm glad that you are enjoying yourself. I can't believe you've joined a poetry club – I laughed a lot. If you send me your poem, I'll read it. Then I can tell you if you should read it out. Can I come to visit you next weekend? I'd like to meet Sophie and I'd like to watch you at the poetry slam.
CU next week I hope
Paul

Unit 5

1 **across:** 1. orches**t**ra; 5. vocal**s**; 6. so**n**gwriter; 10. **mus**icia**n**; 11. opera
down: 2. h**i**t; 3. recorde**r**; 4. ba**s**s; 6. st**u**dent; 7. gui**t**ari**s**t; 8. rapp**e**r; 9. pia**n**o
Lösungswort: instruments

2 1. keyboard; 2. encyclopedia; 3. music stand; 4. vest; 5. record; 6. hospital

3 I love **classical** music – I love to try and hear the different **instruments** which are playing in the orchestra. I also like reggae and **rock** and I was really glad to hear that U2, my favourite rock band, is going on **tour** next year and they are coming to my town.
As soon as I heard they were coming I went to **queue** outside the **ticket office** – with hundreds of other people – and with my **guitar.** I know all the **lyrics** to Bono's songs, of course, and I played a few while I was waiting. The people around me liked it and that, I hope, was the start of my **career** as a musician.

4 1. You weren't very polite. You were **rude.**
2. If you're mad, you could be crazy or you could just be **angry.**
3. If you need a drink, then you're **thirsty.**
4. When you win lots of things, you're **successful.**
5. People who are nice to other people are **kind.**
6. Something that you can do is **possible.**
7. Something that you would like to forget is **embarrassing.**
8. If you have not got enough money, then you are **poor.**

5 I don't like that game. It's **unplayable.**
That book is terrible. It's **unreadable.**
That's a special glass. It's **unbreakable.**
That was a great party. It was very **enjoyable.**
The police have problems with some mysteries. They are **unsolvable.**
That mountain isn't very high. It's **climbable.**
I made a cake but it was **uneatable.**

6 1. a piece of paper; 2. a piece of information; 3. a piece of music; 4. two pieces of furniture

7 *Man:* Are you lost? **Can I help you?**
Woman: Yes please. Can you tell me how to get to the waterfront museum?
Man: Yes, I can show you the way if you like.
Woman: **That's very kind of you.**

Girl: I'm terrible sorry if I hurt you yesterday.
Girl: **I didn't mean to be rude.**

8
1. I can understand the actors there very well.
2. We needn't sit in our seats all the time.
3. You must buy a ticket.
4. We mustn't/can't take photos.

9 How much are the tickets, please?
What time does the concert start?
Can I buy two tickets, please?

10
1. How many singles have you sold?
2. When are you going to make your next CD?
3. Which/What instruments can you play?
4. How often do you practise?
5. Were you good at music when you were a child?
6. What did you do last weekend?

11 You like music, **don't you?**
John can't sing at all, **can he?**
You haven't got the new CD already, **have you?**
Beyoncé has played here a few times, **hasn't she?**
He had problems with drugs, **didn't he?**

12 Shall I carry them for you?
Shall I make you a cup of tea?
Shall I sing it now?

13 There's good film on at the cinema. – Shall we go and watch it?
You want to sing a new song with your band. – Shall we write one?
You're hungry.– Shall we buy a sandwich?
You're tired. – Shall we get the bus home?

14 Jenny can't remember the lyrics.
David needn't sing.
They all must practise a lot.
John may not/can't/mustn't practise the drums at home.

15 1. b); 2. a); 3. c)

16 1. When I was five, I wasn't able to sing.
2. I had to be quiet when my parents listened to music.
3. I wasn't allowed to play the piano very loudly.
4. I didn't have to have music lessons.
5. I was allowed to play my mum's piano.

17 We've had a great holiday and lots of things have been different. Usually when we buy things in the shops, we needn't think too hard but here we**'ve had to** try hard to understand people. Usually we can understand everything on TV but we **haven't been able to** in England. Usually we must go to bed early but on holiday we **haven't had to** go to bed before 11 pm. And usually we can't get up late – our mother doesn't let us stay in bed after 7 am – but on holiday we**'ve been allowed to** stay in bed until lunchtime. But on holiday we've wanted to get up early.

18 I'll be able to come home when I want to.
I'll be allowed to cook the food which I want to eat.
But maybe I won't be able to cook it?
I won't have to do any homework but I will have to work.
I won't be allowed to go to school any more. What a pity!

19 When I was a child, I was able to sing very loudly.
I have never had to use a microphone to fill a concert hall.
I hope I'll be allowed to sing in operas when I'm 70.

20 I meet my friend, Alan, **while** I am waiting for the bus into town. He tells me **that** there is a concert outside in the park this afternoon. He asks me **if** I want to go, too. It is a band that I don't like **but** I want to go **because** I like concerts – and Alan. I'll go **as long as/if** it's not too expensive.
It's 1 pm and the concert doesn't start **until** four. We decide to buy tickets first. **After/When** we've bought them, we go to a café in town **and** buy a drink. **When** we finish our drinks, it's 3 pm, **so** we walk slowly to the park. **When/As soon as** we get there it starts to rain, **but** it doesn't matter; it's the best concert I've ever been to.

21 1. They all still play.

22 1. Boomtown Rats; 2. Bob Geldof; 3. Frank Farian; 4. Rolling Stones; 5. Boney M.; 6. Bob Geldof; 7. Boney M.

23
1. **Although** Geldof played with a successful band, he became really famous when he started Band Aid. **After** Geldof had been successful with Band Aid, he organized Live Aid. Live Aid was very famous **because** it took place in New York and London at the same time
2. Mick Jagger and Keith Richards became leaders of the Rolling Stones **because** they wrote most of the songs. **Before** the Rolling Stones became famous in the States, they were successful in Great Britain. You can still see the Rolling Stones **but** without all of their first members.
3. **While** Frank Farian was working as a singer himself, he started his new band Boney M. He sang at least two voices in the songs **but** other people went on stage for him.

24 1. her; 2. tour; 3. jazz; 4. vest; 5. live

25

1.

Woman 1: Those bags look very heavy. Can I help you?
Woman 2: Well, I'm just going home and you're going into town, aren't you?
Woman 1: I'm not in a hurry. So it's no problem. I can take them home for you if you like.
Woman 2: That's very kind of you. Thanks.

2.

Boy 1: Could you open that door for me, please?
Boy 2: Yes, of course.
Boy 1: Thanks a lot. I've hurt my arm and I can't open it myself.
Boy 2: That's no problem.

3.

Boy: Hi.
Girl: Hi Richard. How are you?
Boy: OK.
Girl: Look. I'm very sorry about yesterday.
Boy: Don't worry about it.
Girl: I didn't mean to be rude.

1. b); 2. c); 3. b)

26 *Girl:* What's the matter?
Boy: Oh, Joey's lost his voice.
Girl: Joey?
Boy: Yes, you know. He sings in our band. And we've got a concert on Saturday. It's our first one and we really wanted to play.
Girl: Oh no. So what are you going to do? Have you found somebody else?
Boy: No, we haven't been able to yet. We're still looking for somebody. Can you sing?
Girl: Well, I can sing in the bathroom.
Boy: Will you help us then?
Girl: No. I won't be able to sing in front of lots of people.
Boy: Well, you'll just have to close your eyes and imagine you're in the bathroom.
Girl: Ha ha. And anyway I don't know the songs.
Boy: I'll go and get the lyrics now.
Girl: No. Stop. I won't be able to learn so many songs before Saturday, will I?
Boy: You will. Most of the songs you know already. We're just going to do some famous songs and then a few of our own songs.
Girl: I didn't know that you wrote your own songs. Why don't you sing them at the school disco?
Boy: We aren't allowed to sing them at school.
Girl: Why not? They aren't rude, are they?
Boy: Well ...
Girl: Oh OK. I'll do it.

1. a); 2. b); 3. c); 4. a); 5. c); 6. a)

27 1. Pete; 2. Pete; 3. Pete; 4. Jenny; 5. Jenny

28 I won't be able to sing in front of lots of people.
You'll just have to close your eyes and imagine you're in the bathroom.
We aren't allowed to sing them at school.
I won't be able to learn so many songs before Saturday, will I?

Skills workshop 5

1

A. text message
B. note
C. diary
D. e-mail
E. rhyme/lyrics

2

1. D; 2. B; 3. C; 4. A; 5. E; 6. H; 7. F; 8. G

3

10 Barton Road
Winchcombe
GL4 5PT

10th June

Dear Steffen,
Thanks for your letter. It was great to hear from you again. I'd love to meet you again. You don't need a hotel because you can stay with us. We have enough room.
I think the end of August is the best time to come to London. Then we can go to the Notting Hill Carnival. That's great and you shouldn't miss it. The weather is usually good in August, too. There are lots of things to do in London but I think one of the best things is the Science Museum. I think you should stay in London for two weeks at least.
Yes, the skiing holiday was great. I haven't been skiing since then, but I'd like to try it again some time. I hope you're well.

Best wishes,
Daniel

Test practice C

1 before: factories, industry, rain, football
after: festivals, music, rain, interesting places, students

2

Didsbury:	You can see things, listen to music, go to pubs or cafés.
Blackpool:	You can ride on ponies, listen to music or watch beach theatre. You can visit the piers, Blackpool Tower and the Pleasure Beach and go on the ghost train.
Edale:	You can walk, climb, ride horses or go camping or mountain-biking.

3 1. b); 2. b); 3. b); 4. c); 5. a)

4 fun: lustig, spaßig – from "fun" *(Substantiv)*
seaside: Küste – from "sea" and "side"
ponies: Ponys – *wie im Deutschen*
theme park: Themenpark – *ähnlich wie im Deutschen*

5
1. It's true **that** ...: Konjunktion
2. OK, I know **that** ...: Konjunktion
3. ... the music was so good **that** we didn't even notice **that** it was ...: 2x Konjunktion
4. ... you can visit **that** aren't ...: Relativpronomen
5. ... the Pennines. **That** are the mountains ...: Demonstrativpronomen

6

Father:	Gibt es besondere Preise für Kinder oder Familien?
You:	**Are there special prices for children or families?**
Assistant:	Yes, it's half the price for children under sixteen.
You:	**Ja, für Kinder unter sechzehn kostet es die Hälfte.**
Mother:	Frag ihn, ob wir Fotos machen dürfen.
You:	**Are we allowed to/May we/Can we take photos?**
Assistant:	No, you can't but you can buy photos in the shop.
You:	**Nein, aber man kann welche im Laden kaufen.**

7 *Woman:* Hello, can I help you?
Man: Oh yes, please. We'd like to see some of the area around Manchester. Do you have any information about it?
Woman: Oh yes. We've got lots of information. Where would you like to go most, to a beach or to the mountains or to an interesting town?
Man: Hm, the weather's so beautiful at the moment; we'd like to go to the beach.
Woman: Well, you can go to Blackpool – Blackpool's very famous – or Southport, which is a bit quieter or ...
Man: Is Blackpool far away?
Woman: No, it's not so far. In the car it's about 40 minutes or just over an hour on the train.
Man: Is the train expensive?
Woman: I'm not sure. You'll need to ask at the station or you can get tickets online, of course.
Man: Thanks a lot.

1. the tourist/the man; 2. the woman/the assistant; 3. the beach/Blackpool; 4. quieter than Blackpool; 5. at the station or online

8 Tübingen is a student town and there's a lot to do there all year. In winter you can go to the Christmas market or go skiing in the Swabian Alb which are mountains not far away. In summer you can go on boats on the river and walk or cycle in the beautiful country around the town. It is also a great place for music, concerts and festivals. There are music, film and food festivals all through the year.

Bildquellennachweis:

S. 6: Picture-Alliance (dpa), Frankfurt; Picture-Alliance (Rebeca Naden), Frankfurt; Corbis (Duomo), Düsseldorf; Getty Images (MN Chan), München
S. 9: Alamy Images RM (Janine Wiedel), Abingdon, Oxon
S. 18: Picture-Alliance (Rebeca Naden), Frankfurt; MEV Verlag GmbH, Augsburg; Avenue Images GmbH (Image 100), Hamburg
S. 22: Marco Polo Agence Photographique (F. Bouillot), Paris
S. 29: Fotolia LLC (RF/Jason Stitt), New York
S. 30: Avenue Images GmbH (Image Source), Hamburg; Alamy Images RM (AA World Travel), Abingdon, Oxon; Ullstein Bild GmbH (Spiegl), Berlin; Corel Corporation Deutschland, Unterschleissheim
S. 32: Getty Images RF, München; Fotosearch Stock Photography (PhotoDisc), Waukesha, WI; MEV Verlag GmbH, Augsburg
S. 84: terre des hommes Deutschland e.V., Osnabrück
S. 99: Corbis, Düsseldorf
S. 100: AKG (Rainer Hackenberg), Berlin
S. 101: Europa-Farbbildarchiv Klammet; Mauritius Images, Mittenwald.

Der Verlag hat sich nach bestem Wissen und Gewissen bemüht, alle Inhaber von Urheberrechten an Texten und Abbildungen zu diesem Werk ausfindig zu machen. Sollte das in irgendeinem Fall nicht korrekt geschehen sein, bitten wir um Entschuldigung und bieten an, gegebenenfalls in einer nachfolgenden Auflage einen korrigierten Quellennachweis zu bringen.